# The *It's Not About the Sex* Workbook

This intimate guide offers readers step-by-step suggestions to build traction and create momentum in any stage of healing through illuminating case studies, memoir snapshots, as well as applicable action steps.

The book presents a forward-thinking wellness model that takes the whole person into consideration rather than pathologizing or dwelling on compulsive behavior of the past. Each chapter includes a composite case study and a memoir snapshot to set the tone and illustrate themes to be explored. The studies and snapshots demonstrate the residual challenges and limitless opportunities facing those in long-term recovery from sexual compulsivity. Utilizing the tools of positive psychology, attachment theory, and nervous system regulation, readers are challenged to leverage their resilience and resourcefulness. Critical issues such as spirituality and mindfulness provide a purposeful soul-searching toward wellness and well-being.

For use in conjunction with therapy, twelve-step groups or as a self-help workbook, this book focuses on the present and the future with an emphasis on the establishment of deeper connection and cultivating greater life fulfilment beyond compulsive sexual behavior.

**Andrew Susskind, LCSW, SEP, CGP**, is a psychotherapist in private practice in Los Angeles, California. He is the author of several books, including *It's Not About the Sex: Moving from Isolation to Intimacy after Sexual Addiction* (2019).

# The *It's Not About the Sex* Workbook

Moving from Isolation to Intimacy After Sexual Compulsivity

**Andrew Susskind**

Routledge
Taylor & Francis Group

NEW YORK AND LONDON

First published 2024
by Routledge
605 Third Avenue, New York, NY 10158

and by Routledge
4 Park Square, Milton Park, Abingdon, Oxon, OX14 4RN

*Routledge is an imprint of the Taylor & Francis Group, an informa business*

ISBN: 978-1-032-65046-3 (pbk)
ISBN: 978-1-032-65048-7 (ebk)

DOI: 10.4324/9781032650487

Typeset in ITC Galliard Pro
by Newgen Publishing UK

To all my teachers, past and present.

# Contents

# Introduction

After years of deliberation, the World Health Organization now recognizes *Compulsive Sexual Behavior Disorder* (CSBD) in the *International Classification of Diseases*. This is the first time in history that CSBD has been validated by a global gathering of clinicians. Although I don't agree with the pathologizing nature of naming this behavior a disorder or a disease, it creates a path toward advanced research and deeper understanding for this ongoing mental health challenge.

For many years Certified Sex Addiction Therapists (CSATs) have lobbied to include *sex addiction* as a formal diagnosis, but to no avail. The often-misunderstood term was coined by Patrick Carnes in the 1980s, but it has always been a controversial and misinterpreted label accepted by some and rejected by others.

Here is a brief scenario that opened my eyes to the need for further clinical exploration and public education. My client, "Deborah," is now in her late fifties, and she shared the story of her sexual abuse perpetrated by a male high school teacher. After that event, Deborah became dangerously promiscuous both as a teenager and throughout her young adulthood. She felt profoundly isolated with the secret of her abuse as well as her sexually compulsive behavior. When she was in high school there were scarce resources, and she didn't know where to seek help. Deborah explained to me that a book with *sex addiction* in the title would not fully capture the complexity of her pain and trauma, but if *compulsive sex* was part of the title, she would have picked up the book.

Regardless of how these behaviors are described, getting the most effective support is always the highest mental health priority, but Deborah's fresh perspective opened my eyes to the range of trauma that often goes along with sexual compulsivity. In addition to those who have found recovery in the twelve-step rooms, there are many others who have experienced out-of-control sexual behaviors who never made it to a twelve-step meeting or therapy.

As someone who feels eternally grateful for my twelve-step communities, I've always leaned toward the term *sexually compulsive* rather than *sex addict* for several reasons. The model for sexual addiction was borrowed from Alcoholics Anonymous, and the *Big Book* labels alcoholism as a disease through the lens of the medical model.

Inadvertently, the term "sex addiction" pathologizes the behavior rather than opening a dialogue of curiosity and exploration. Because shame resiliency and

DOI: 10.4324/9781032650487-1

sexual health are such a core part of healing from compulsive sexual behavior, I try to steer away from anything that may identify the problem as a disease or get in the way of restoring sexual wellness.

Professionally, I have always walked a fine line between sex addiction therapists and sex therapists and hold both specialty areas respectfully. What I do bring to the conversation is thirty-two years of personal and professional experience as I now look at the healing process through the lens of attachment repair, trauma healing, and sexual health. There is an ongoing necessity to help clients stop self-destructive behaviors, but unfortunately, there is still a territorial and sometimes competitive nature associated with the existing treatment models. The ICD classification introduces a profound change in the language that describes the brokenheartedness of those like Deborah who may never identify as sex addicts or step into a twelve-step room.

After writing my book *It's Not About the Sex*, it became clear that action steps were needed to move forward in sexual recovery. It's helpful to build awareness and insight, but it's another thing to feel internal and external movement. I decided to infuse this workbook with stories from my own recovery to highlight some of the challenges and opportunities that I face and many of you may face. As always, I'm open to hearing from you about what resonates for you and what doesn't. Give yourself plenty of time as you work through these chapters knowing that recovery is a dynamic trajectory.

There is no right or wrong way to approach this workbook. You might consider focusing on a chapter a week with a friend or a study group keeping in mind this is not a one-size-fits-all process. Because some of the exercises can be activating, pace yourself and ask for support along the way. More than anything, allow yourself to be open-hearted and try to remain curious and nonjudgmental.

## References

Alcoholics Anonymous World Services. 2002. *Big Book*. New York: Alcoholics Anonymous World Services.
Carnes, Patrick. 1983. *Out of the Shadows*. Center City, MN: CompCare.
World Health Organization. 2018. *International Classification of Diseases* (11th ed.).

# 1  Reclaiming Resilience

*I was the baby of the family, the youngest of four boys. It was a complicated upbringing, to say the least; a family starving for love but not a clue how to express it to one another. As a child, I easily fell into the role of being a heat-seeking missile in search of love, attention, and validation wherever I could find it—from best friends, teachers, crossing guards—from anyone who provided more nourishment than home. This is the origin of my brokenheartedness as well as my resilience.*

*Did I go off the tracks as a young adult when I started to look for sex and romance in all the wrong places? Probably, but I knew from a young age that loving relationships were also going to be a sanctuary for me. At age five I was fortunate enough to have a grandmother who moved from Brooklyn to my hometown of Cherry Hill, New Jersey—just in time for me to enter kindergarten. We all need an unconditionally accepting person in our lives to remind us how lovable we truly are. I was extremely fortunate to have someone who showed up that way in my childhood, yet others may need to play catch-up later in life.*

*My emotional resilience was highly disrupted by the constant turbulence at home, yet somehow, I knew that my spirit was still alive, and my job was to reclaim it. My compulsive sexual behavior was a misfired attempt to regulate my nervous system, and since the time I went to my first twelve-step meeting in November 1994, I've been on a road to restoring resilience, resourcefulness, and regulation.*

If you look beneath the compulsive sexual behavior, you will most likely find brokenheartedness in one of the following ways:

- Trauma: specific (car accident, natural disaster, physical injuries)
- Abuse: sexual, physical, emotional, or religious
- Neglect: unintentional or intentional
- Abandonment: parent or caregiver leaving a child
- Grief and Loss: deaths, goodbyes, divorce, relocations, breakups

**Action Step**: This is a heavy question to start off our workbook experience together but take a moment and write about your brokenheartedness. If you're not ready to write about all the details, simply list the events you remember.

_____

_____

_____

DOI: 10.4324/9781032650487-2

According to the World Health Organization, sexual health is defined as "...a state of physical, emotional, mental, and social well-being in relation to sexuality; it is not merely the absence of disease, dysfunction, or infirmity. Sexual health requires a positive and respectful approach to sexuality and sexual relationships, as well as the possibility of having pleasurable and safe sexual experiences, free of coercion, discrimination, and violence. For sexual health to be attained and maintained, the sexual rights of all persons must be respected, protected, and fulfilled."

**Action Step**: Based on this definition of sexual health, what resonates for you and where would you like to place your focus as you move through the exercises in this workbook?

_____

_____

_____

In Chapter Ten we will spend more time exploring how sexual health fits into your overall recovery, but for now we will take a look at how emotional resilience takes shape.

## Jessica's Story: Unlocking the Starting Gate

*Jessica arrived in my office in sheer desperation. After many years of sleeping around and countless broken relationships, she was at the end of her rope. Recently, Jessica became suicidal as she found herself juggling several meaningless sex partners while having unprotected sex with each of them.*

*Growing up in a lower-middle-class family in an affluent town, she always felt inferior to others. Her parents were busy making ends meet, and Jessica was left to her own devices. As a young teenager, she began to receive more attention for her appearance but never did well in school and started having sex at age thirteen with a star high school soccer player. Sex with multiple athletes became her sport. Even though she felt powerful and competent in this arena, this self-destructive pattern continued for many years, leaving her feeling miserable and hollow.*

*At the suggestion of a trusted friend, Jessica grudgingly attended her first Sex and Love Addicts Anonymous meeting. To her surprise, she heard story after story that resembled hers. She realized she was not alone and started going to daily meetings. With the help of a temporary sponsor, she made a painful decision to completely stop contact with all her former sexual partners for the time being, and instead, focus on herself for the first time ever. Jessica has now arrived at the starting gate of her recovery and fortunately found wisdom and guidance from women who have been in her shoes. They have something she wants—resilience and hope.*

Jessica's brokenheartedness doesn't imply that there is anything wrong with her. It means that there is something wrong *around* her—both from her complicated childhood as well as more recent traumatic experiences. Although deep-rooted pain is central to Jessica's story, we will focus on her capacity to move forward in her recovery with emotional resilience.

Brokenheartedness often begins in early childhood within families, neighborhoods, and schools. For example, a seven-year-old boy named Tyler was incessantly bullied by a pack of teenagers because he spent most of his time alone doodling in a sketchbook and was enamored with anything creative. He carried hidden shame but didn't feel comfortable enough to tell his parents for fear that the bullying would increase.

Shameful events illustrate the invisible suffering that can develop later into out-of-control sexual behavior—an attempt to escape feelings of shame. Whether it's the cause or the effect of sexual compulsivity, brokenheartedness is inevitable, and with the right healing and support, can also be a catalyst for sustainable recovery.

**Action Step**: What is your invisible pain, past or present? Write about these experiences that you may or may not have shared with others.

_____

_____

_____

What are your antidotes for brokenheartedness? In other words, what has helped you persevere through the toughest times?

_____

_____

_____

The antidotes to brokenheartedness often show up through intimacy, deeper connection, and emotionally reliable relationships. As part of my own recovery, receiving love has always been the biggest challenge. When I ask others, I almost always get the same answer: "I'm better at giving love than receiving it." In my family of origin, we loved one another but didn't know how to show love to one another. As a result, I remained hungry within the confines of my own home—a heartbreaking, yet common story.

**Action Step:** How would you describe the love in your childhood? Was it abundant? Was it scarce? Was it intermittent? Who were your primary sources of love?

_____

_____

_____

**Action Step**: Where is the love in your life today? List all those sources now.

_____

_____

_____

**Action Step:** Who are the people in your life who seem to withhold their love from you? Make a list of those individuals so you can start to identify where the love flows freely or not. Keep in mind that it's not helpful to go to the hardware store to buy milk.

_____

_____

_____

## Establishing Sexual Boundaries

One of the most challenging questions to ask yourself is "What is compulsive and what is not compulsive?"

**Action Step**: How do you know when you are sexually compulsive?

_____

_____

_____

In twelve-step programs for compulsive sexual behavior, it's recommended that you develop a sexual recovery plan preferably with a sponsor or a therapist specializing in this area. Your recovery plan specifies behaviors you would like to stop (destructive or self-destructive) as well as those you would like to introduce (enriching, healing activities).

*From a twelve-step perspective, sexual sobriety can be defined as "learning to be sexual without it becoming obsessive, compulsive or out of control." How do you define your sexual boundaries currently?*

_____

_____

_____

**Action Step**: If you don't have a written plan, ask yourself the following questions, "Are my current sexual behaviors destructive or depleting? Are they enriching or affirming?" This can be a litmus test to determine healthier sexual choices. List those behaviors that are life-depleting and those that are life-enriching:

*Depleting behaviors:*

_____

_____

_____

*Enriching behaviors:*

_____

_____

_____

Emotional resilience can only take shape once you are sexually sober. Begin by identifying a trusted confidant such as a sponsor, therapist, or close friend, and practice taking emotional risks.

**Action Step:** How would you like to be more emotionally vulnerable with others? What would be one small step that would make the biggest difference?

_____

_____

_____

Once you begin to take emotional risks by sharing more with others, you will become more emotionally accessible and greater trust will take shape. In the past you may have learned to keep your deepest thoughts and emotions to yourself, but moving beyond secrecy toward meaningful connection is fundamental to resilience. Now that we've explored brokenheartedness and sexual sobriety, here are the central characteristics of emotional resilience:

- The capacity to experience the fullness of life.
- A resilient, resourceful, regulated state of well-being.
- When you feel most like yourself (comfortable in your skin).

**Action Step:** Because there are many ways to describe Emotional Resilience, how would you like to define it? Keep your definition where you can see it— post-it on the refrigerator, near your computer, or in your phone.

_____

_____

_____

### Locating the 4 Rs of Emotional Resilience: Relax, Regulate, Respond, Relate

Here are the 4 Rs of emotional resilience and action steps to support each of them:

1. *Relax:* How do you relax? Not simply vegging in front of the television but physiologically relaxing. **Action Step:** Name two to three ways you can commit to relax.
2. *Regulate:* When you're dysregulated, you may notice rage, panic, disconnection, or depression. When you're regulated, you'll feel calm, grounded, and peaceful. One form of nervous system regulation is through grounding. **Action Step:** Sit in a comfortable chair and notice your breath. Just observe it. Then notice the weight of your body being supported by the chair—both the seat as well as the back. Observe your feet connected to the ground beneath you. Notice what's happening inside of you—any thoughts, feelings, or sensations. Stay mindful of your body and your breath for approximately one minute as you begin to ground yourself. Repeat as desired.
3. *Respond:* When you react impulsively, you automatically feel ungrounded. Here are a few simple action steps to respond rather than react:

   - Pause.
   - Observe your breath.
   - Notice what's happening in your body.
   - Bite your tongue.

   **Action Step:** What are a few ways you are willing to respond rather than react?

   _____

   _____

   _____

Let's take a deeper look at responding rather than reacting. You had a long day at work and your friend calls to let you know they are disappointed that you haven't stayed in touch recently even though you knew their father died last month. You're feeling criticized and immediately feel shame. This is a typical emotional reaction, but how can you respond?

First, you might consider biting your tongue. Instead of saying the first thing on your mind, ground yourself and take a deep breath. This will buy some time and allow you to pause and regulate. Secondly, try not to take it personally, but instead, have compassion for your friend as well as yourself. They are simply expressing their feelings and you can be grateful that they feel safe enough to share honestly with you. Lastly, notice your body and do your best to breathe and relax. If not right away, hold the intention for your nervous system to regulate.

It's the human condition to react when something feels threatening. We also have the capacity to respond—if not immediately, then soon thereafter. Ask yourself if you really need to say something or if it may be an opportunity to simply listen and understand your friend's feelings. There is no right or wrong about such charged interactions but responding rather than reacting leaves you with more productive and loving options.

4. *Relate*: Cultivate connectedness. Here are three primary sources of connection:

- Connection to self.
- Connection to trusted others.
- Connection to a power greater than oneself.

**Action Step:** List two to three ways you can connect to yourself daily.

_____

_____

_____

**Action Step:** List two to three ways you can connect with a trustworthy person.

_____

_____

_____

**Action Step:** List two to three ways you can connect with something greater than yourself (higher power, universal energy, nature).

_____

_____

_____

In summary, the more you practice emotional resilience skills daily, the less likely you will rely on out-of-control sexual behavior. These skills are meant to be a practice—like a fire drill. Practice the 4 Rs as often as you brush your teeth— relax, regulate, respond, relate. Lean into the love around you and observe yourself without judgment as you integrate resilience into your healing direction.

## Expanding Emotional Resilience

I've always liked the word "resilience." Maybe it's how the word itself sounds or maybe it's what it means to me, but it has always resonated powerfully. Resilience can be a superpower that shows up when life's greatest challenges get thrown in your direction. It also reveals the perseverance of the human spirit to bounce back from extraordinary circumstances.

Trauma can be described as *something that happens that is too much or too fast to process at the time*. As a result, your brain can't integrate the deep impact of the event, which often results in dysregulation such as rage, panic, disconnection, or shutting down. Resilience is essential for those in recovery because chronic dysregulation leaves you at higher risk for ongoing problematic sexual choices.

*When I grew up in the 70s in a suburb of Philadelphia, every fourth home had the same basic blueprint. It was a typical cookie-cutter neighborhood which was the modern design at the time, and it was safe and affordable by most standards. Yet, inside my home, it wasn't so safe. Although I don't believe there was malicious intent, my family was emotionally volatile and scary at times. My developing nervous system walked on eggshells, and as a result, I became a heat-seeking missile—seeking safer ground wherever I found it. A best friend was always part of my survival strategy, and in turn, I was generously adopted by several kindhearted families along the way. My version of resilience propelled me to seek safety, connection, and love outside the home. Eventually, this evolved into looking for love in all the wrong places: compulsive sex, obsession, and fantasy.*

**Action Step**: Reflect on your childhood years and identify examples of resilience.

_____

_____

_____

Resilience often reveals itself amid trauma or from life's hurts, disappointments, or shame experiences. In other words, resilience is an inner resource of the human condition and the human spirit. Nowadays I look back on my childhood with bittersweet memories, but I remain grateful that my capacity to bounce back from adversity is based on the trauma and dysregulation I experienced as a kid. Not everyone is so fortunate.

## Brian's Story: Taking the Road to Resilience

*Brian finished his third round of rehab at age twenty-eight. Although he has never sustained a relationship with a girlfriend, he has a long-term relationship with alcohol and benzos, as well as paying for sex; and he never found traction academically, socially, or professionally. Brian was the oldest of three siblings and always felt responsible for his younger sisters. His father worked long hours in finance and drank heavily, especially on the weekends. His mother was a medical social worker who always appeared highly anxious and spent more time focusing on her clients than her own family. After his youngest sister died suddenly in a car accident, Brian felt extreme shame for not protecting her.*

*As a child, Brian over functioned as he became a third parent, but he couldn't save his sister from her fate. In spite of the excruciating grief and sorrow, he always tried to stay on track with his recovery as he consistently showed up to twelve-step meetings and is now interested in immersing himself in a new sobriety plan—moving into a sober living home, twice a week therapy, and working the steps with a sponsor. When*

*I asked him what was going to be different this time around, he shared a common sentiment: "I'm sick and tired of being sick and tired." When someone is depleted, it can either be a moment of awakening—truly doing whatever it takes to move forward—or it can be more of the same suffering. This window of opportunity could give Brian new tools to practice the skills of emotional resilience.*

Brian's story is all too common. Will his resilience be strong enough to help him through this precarious time? Resilience is a daily practice like going to the gym, and it's about building muscle toward a more regulated nervous system.

**Action Step**: What are you willing to do to build your emotional resilience? (For example, texting a friend instead of isolating, going to a meeting when you don't feel like it, meditating and praying no matter what).

_____

_____

_____

We all face adversity, and we also build resilience through adversity. The following practices, tools, and strategies promote nervous system regulation, resilience, and resourcefulness. As a result, you will feel more buoyant regardless of life's obstacles.

**Action Step**: Learn about your nervous system. The goal is to feel more regulated more of the time. Monitor when you are feeling calm, grounded, and peaceful and when you are not. Pay attention to the shift from dysregulation to regulation and savor the moments when you are feeling more resilient. Check in with yourself right now. Are you feeling calm, grounded, and peaceful? If not, what are you feeling internally at this moment?

_____

_____

_____

**Action Step:** Practice Mindful Self-Compassion every day–either through a guided meditation or through positive self-talk. Consider short meditations available on my website or consider Chris Germer or Tara Brach on YouTube as morning tone setters. If you're having a difficult moment, take a few minutes to practice self-kindness such as taking a few deep breaths, going on a walk, or getting yourself a cup of tea. The more you practice self-compassion, the more resilience grows. Identify two to three acts of self-kindness you will consider when you're in self-attack mode.

_____

_____

_____

**Action Step**: Build capacity for contentment and gratitude. To counterbalance pain or distress, capture moments of calm and contentment. Notice when you are feeling more regulated and savor it. By practicing gratitude throughout your day, you'll begin to carve fresh-new neural pathways resulting in a higher likelihood for resilience. Begin now by listing three to five current examples of gratitude.

_____

_____

_____

An ideal space to work on shame resilience is in a therapy group, whether it be in-person or online. Brené Brown reminds us that "shame is given to us by others and shame is healed through others," and group therapy is an exceptional opportunity to heal your deepest shame while feeling less alone. Shame resilience can be a healing result of any group experience including twelve-step meetings, support groups, or group therapy.

In addition to Chapter Six in *It's Not About the Sex*, read as much as you can about the nervous system. Self-knowledge is not only empowering, but it also helps your brain understand and integrate information about trauma and the healing process. Consider David Grand's *Brainspotting* and Peter Levine's *Waking the Tiger*, in addition to others.

**Action Step**: Keep a daily resilience journal taking note of any moments or experiences of resilience—big or small. For now, write a resilience inventory any time you transcend a highly challenging experience. Include how this felt to you during and after these events.

_____

_____

_____

**Action Step**: Identify the emotionally reliable, unconditionally loving people in your life. They are nonjudgmental, curious, and always in your corner.

_____

_____

_____

If you're unable to name anyone, it's never too late to start the search. When you surround yourself with dependable people, you will feel less anxiety and more resilience. Double up on your contact with trusted people and let them know they are part of your resilience team.

**Action Step**: Consider what gives your life meaning and purpose. Positive Psychologists believe that engagement and meaning are two of the pillars of life fulfillment. Without overthinking it, what gives your life meaning now? (We will explore this further in Chapter Eight). If you're not sure yet, take a guess and start to play with the possibilities. Remember that it may be right in front of you (for example, being the best parent you can be).

_____

_____

_____

**Action Step**: As you contemplate purpose as part of your recovery, how would you describe your current relationship with a Power Greater than Yourself? Take stock of this spiritual connection. If you're inclined to contemplate some type of spiritual connection, resilience will inevitably grow.

_____

_____

_____

The action steps and skills in this chapter are meant to be practiced as part of your ongoing healing strategies. Choose which of these tools fit best for you and find an accountability partner to practice them on a regular basis. As you pay attention to your resilience levels, take note of your nervous system and how you respond to these strategies. Observe your resilience level with curiosity and non-judgment.

## Your Practice

1. Identify your brokenheartedness—an act of self-compassion. Track your heartbreak both from the past and in the present as you let your wounds heal.
2. Begin to consider what sexual wellness means to you. Give yourself plenty of time and space to consider the many possibilities available to you.
3. Clarify your sexual boundaries, which will give you parameters to decide what's working and what's not working. Enlist the help of trusted others.
4. Emotional resilience can be described as the 4 Rs: Relax, Regulate, Respond, and Relate. Incorporate these awareness tools daily.
5. Resilience shows up through emotional regulation and leads to buoyancy and shame resilience. Take note of when you're feeling resilient.
6. Gratitude journals have become mainstream, whether it be on paper or in your head. Keep a resilience journal to track the way you are navigating recovery.

## References

Brown, Brené. 2010. *The Gifts of Imperfection: Let Go of Who You Think You're Supposed to Be and Embrace Who You Are.* Center City, MN: Hazelden.

Grand, David. 2013. *Brainspotting: The Revolutionary New Therapy for Rapid and Effective Change.* Louisville, CO: Sounds True.

Levine, Peter. 1997. *Waking the Tiger: Healing Trauma.* Berkeley, CA: North Atlantic Books.

World Health Organization. "Sexual and Reproductive Health and Research (SRH)." www.who.int/teams/sexual-and-reproductive-health-and-research-(srh)/areas-of-work/sexual-health.

# 2  Living with Loss

*I was a* Sesame Street *kid. The groundbreaking, culture-shifting TV show premiered just after my fifth birthday, and I was transfixed. A multi-cultural street where everyone seemed to get along, and even when they didn't, they seemed to actually listen to one another and work things out. I was lost in the depth and kindness of these characters—Bert and Ernie, Cookie Monster, Oscar the Grouch, and of course, Big Bird. They became my first fantasy family and a focal point of clean fun and pure imagination.*

*Outside the Public Broadcasting System, home was not so idyllic. Instead, there were heated arguments, vicious fighting, and fierce competition, with a lot of envy and palpable shame in the mix. Somehow, I held on to the hope that we could work things out just like they seemed to do so naturally on* Sesame Street, *but this rarely happened. The arguments became louder. The isolation became more profound, and I learned to get my emotional needs met elsewhere mostly with the loving generosity of my friend's families that adopted me.*

*Every child dreams of a family that gets along and enjoys being together, but this wasn't my experience. When I think back on the idea of a peaceful home, I simply wanted a sanctuary where I would feel safe and protected. Instead, I resourcefully learned how to get lost in the* Wonderful World of Disney *or* Sesame Street *or my friends' seemingly harmonious homes. Back in the 90s my therapist, Darlene, helped me uncover my family trauma as I began to grieve the loss of the fantasy while moving toward accepting the reality of my troubled family. It was time for me to come to terms with the losses of my childhood.*

## Making Peace with Grief

In American culture, most people try to avoid loss altogether, and yet, grieving is a portal toward deeper learning. It not only provides a way to say goodbye, but it also opens the possibility of integrating the loss, lifting the heaviness, and moving forward. If you don't grieve, it gets in the way of processing an ending and in turn creates a blockage of feelings. There is a common myth that you are supposed to get over loss; actually, it's not about getting over it, it's learning to live with it. And fully grieving our losses makes room for more vitality.

As you make your way through this chapter, pace yourself, knowing that grief can be surprisingly exhausting and heartbreaking at times. Give yourself plenty of time and space for self-acceptance, self-compassion, and self-love.

DOI: 10.4324/9781032650487-3

All trauma results in a sense of helplessness—a trapped feeling leaving you with no options. Grief and loss can be traumatic, but it doesn't have to be. If it's swept under the rug, it ignores the brokenheartedness and often festers. If you process the grief and lean into the love around you, it won't linger. By approaching loss head-on, it may even help you feel more capable and competent as you walk through the loss intact. Grief is not a choice, but *how* you grieve is a choice.

**Action Step:** Write about three of your greatest losses. They may be specifically related to your compulsive sexual behavior or not. While you're taking stock of these losses, try not to overthink it—simply start with the losses that stand out for you.

_____

_____

_____

If grief has been something you avoided in the past, consider its value in your recovery. Because grief and loss are inevitable, you have two choices: 1. Ignore it, or 2. Observe it with curiosity and make peace with it. Delving deeper into your grief can be scary at first but also a courageous move toward understanding the true impact of loss on you.

Grief and loss are both intellectual concepts, but if we break them down, they are filled with a variety of feelings including sorrow, anger, love as well as joy. Don't think that grief is only about sadness because it's more complex than that. Let's begin by taking a look at how you have processed losses in the past.

**Action Step:** How would you describe your relationship with grief in the past? In other words, how have you approached losses in your life?

_____

_____

_____

**Action Step:** How would you like your relationship with grief to be in the future? In other words, how would you like to approach losses from now on?

_____

_____

_____

Keep in mind that grief and loss go hand in hand with recovery from problematic sexual behaviors, and I invite you to consider grieving as a growth opportunity from this point forward. There is no right or wrong way to grieve, but acknowledging the loss is the first step. In Jewish tradition there is a mourning ritual where close family "sits shiva" for seven days. After the loss of a loved one, it becomes a time devoted to emotional and spiritual healing where family mourns together and honors the memory of the deceased.

**Action Step:** How would you like to "sit shiva" for your sexual compulsivity? Fully processing losses takes more than seven days, but giving yourself as much space and time to grieve the losses is an act of self-compassion.

_____

_____

_____

As part of recovery, the absence of loved ones can be more pronounced. The loss may have been to death, a break-up, or possibly an estrangement, and these losses often become more real after compulsive behaviors end. Maybe the loss is related to family or friends who are still stuck in their addictive, compulsive behaviors? Don't ignore the empty chair at the dinner table representing someone you loved. It's a reminder that part of moving forward with your life is also about acknowledging and processing the loss.

**Action Step:** Who is missing from your table?

_____

_____

_____

Even though both of my parents died many years ago, their spirits are always with me. Nowadays I try to honor their memories on birthdays, anniversaries, and during family gatherings with a funny story; or I might simply light a memory candle. If the loss is related to a breakup or someone who abandoned you, make room for the feelings of hurt and resentment because you don't want to bypass any of your feelings. It may also be time to express gratitude for what they brought to your life. And if someone is still addicted, hold them in your heart with lovingkindness and healing thoughts.

**Action Step:** How do you remember and honor the memory of loved ones?

_____

_____

_____

Because compulsive behavior is often a way to escape feelings, you may find yourself feeling raw or awkward without participating in mood-altering behaviors.

Because compulsive behavior is a misfired attempt to regulate your nervous system—sometimes to feel more and sometimes to feel less—it is a short-term strategy that isn't sustainable. Practice social connection and fellowship with those you trust and respect. Then you can expand from there and track how it feels to put yourself in more social situations.

**Action Step:** Pace yourself knowing that there is no cookie-cutter approach to connecting with others. You get to choose how much, how little, and with whom you want to invest your energy. Find a balance. Try not to go beyond your capacity and don't hibernate, either. Who would you like to lean on and connect with after a loss?

_____

_____

_____

## Breaking Up with Your Compulsive Past

You were involved in a long-term committed relationship with the sexually compulsive part of you, and now is the time to break up for once and for all. By choosing to end this depleting relationship, you'll make room for renewed relationships, rediscovered interests, and reclaimed vitality. Acknowledging and letting go of compulsive behaviors and fantasies opens up energy for deeper connection. As you mourn the wasted years, you'll discover new-found time, energy, and spirit that naturally emerges. Accepting loss as a natural aspect of recovery will help you learn to *live with it* rather than buying into the myth of *getting over it*.

How do you want to say goodbye to your compulsive behavior? Rather than a one-and-done process, it tends to be a gradual process over time.

**Action Step:** Write a goodbye letter to the sexual compulsion. Part 1: Express gratitude to this part of you. In other words, list the ways that your problematic sexual behavior served a purpose. Part 2: Say goodbye for once and for all to compulsive sexual behavior. For example, I know that out-of-control sexual behavior was a survival strategy that helped me cope with a troubled family. It's an act of faith and courage to say goodbye to a long-term habit even if it doesn't serve you anymore. Take a moment to reflect on this brave decision.

_____

_____

_____

**Action Step:** If you have already stopped engaging in problematic sexual behaviors, what made it possible for you to stop engaging in them? In other words, what shifted internally that told you it was time to move on?

_____

_____

_____

## Mike's Story: Grieving the Loss of the Fantasy

*By the time Mike made it into therapy, he had been involved in twelve-step programs for eight years and thought he was on the right track. For the most part, his life was going along beautifully. At the age of thirty-six, he was the vice president of a local bank and was happily married with two young children. Everything was looking good on the outside, but his insides were eroding.*

*While working with a sponsee on the eighth and ninth steps (i.e., the amends steps) he had a memory of his mother crying uncontrollably, and in retrospect realized that his father had been having an affair with a co-worker. Mike had been idealizing his parents and was holding the idea that his family was perfect as well. Now he realized this wasn't the case.*

*In therapy we explored the notion that all kids have magical thinking and want to see their families as flawless. Somewhere in adulthood it becomes clear that parents are human and make mistakes. Families are imperfect and require understanding and compassion. In the midst of these realizations, grief surfaced for Mike along with feelings of deep sadness, anger, and disillusionment. Mike's blind spots were now illuminated, leaving him feeling raw and vulnerable. Although painful, this is an opportunity to face the losses while at the same time asking for a shoulder to lean on. As Mike learns about this part of himself, he will modify the false family story—a brave and powerful internal shift.*

Childhood loss is often a core element of the brokenheartedness of sexual compulsivity. I always wanted the *Sesame Street* version of my home, but unfortunately, my experience was starkly different. Every child wants a happy family, and the gaps between fantasy and reality can feel insurmountable. Grieving the losses of childhood has been a game-changer in my healing process, and I welcome you to take your time with this section and lean into the love and hugs available to you as you explore it.

**Action Step**: Do you have any memories of innocence and ease in your childhood? If so, name these memories. How old were you when your childhood innocence faded?

_____

_____

_____

*I don't have many memories of an innocent childhood. I know there must have been a few times when I was quite young, but I remember always being the "little adult"; taking things way too seriously and trying to be the glue of the family which was an impossible task for a child. So, I know I missed out on the experiences of fun, freedom, and true relaxation. Don't get me wrong. I was fortunate to have loving friends who were available to do fun things, but my childhood always had a heavy veil over it. When I started kindergarten, my grandmother moved to a neighboring town offering me an unconditionally loving sanctuary in contrast to my turbulent home. Her emotionally reliable presence was a life-saving counterbalance to my chilly home as were loving therapists who have inspired me since I was a teenager.*

**Action Step:** Let's revisit your greatest losses, and this time focus on your primary childhood losses (for example, divorce of parents).

_____

_____

_____

**Action Step:** How have you grieved your childhood losses?

_____

_____

_____

**Action Step:** How would you like to say goodbye to the Norman Rockwell family? I know I am dating myself with this reference, but it refers to an artist who painted idealized versions of families and their celebrations. It's doubtful that anyone reading this book grew up with this type of warm, fuzzy family scene. So, if you haven't said goodbye to this fantasy, now is the time.

_____

_____

_____

**Action Step:** Create a dialogue with your sponsor or therapist about moving from the idealized fantasy toward accepting and living in reality and opening up honest conversations about it.

Embrace your *family of choice*—an authentic, imperfect group of dependable people.

_____

_____

_____

**Action Step:** Who are your dolphins? Those who nourish you, play well, have your back, communicate impeccably, and look after you when you're not feeling well. Identify your dolphins and cultivate these relationships. Let them know you value them and develop ways to have more contact with them.

_____

_____

_____

**Action Step:** Name the people in your life who deplete you.

_____

_____

_____

Maximize the time and energy you give your dolphins and minimize the time and energy you give to those relationships that deplete you. Know that your family of choice will never resemble the Norman Rockwell painting, but it may surprise you and be even better.

One of the greatest losses associated with compulsive sexual behavior is the loss of time, energy, and focus. For example, out-of-control sexual behavior often becomes a part-time job with many hours devoted to compulsive activities each day.

**Action Step:** How many years do you believe you were sexually compulsive?

_____

_____

_____

**Action Step:** What did you miss out on?

_____

_____

_____

**Action Step:** How would you like to utilize your newfound time?

_____

_____

_____

**Action Step:** Now consider ways to reclaim the missed opportunities for being fully engaged in your life. For example, if a nephew was born during the height of your compulsive behavior and you were missing in action, how can you show up more fully for them now? Take stock of what you missed out on and become more mindful of the time and presence you bring to your loved ones today.

_____

_____

_____

One form of grief that gets highlighted in recovery is the gap between what you envisioned in your life and the reality of your current life. The gap may be large or small, but either way it leaves you with lots of feelings including sadness, disappointment, hurt, resentment, and disillusionment, just to name a few.

**Action Step:** Describe in detail how you imagined your life would be at this point. Imagine the little kid inside of you and how you envisioned your grown-up life.

_____

_____

_____

Now acknowledge how your life is different. What is the reality of life today that contrasts with what the little kid imagined?

_____

_____

_____

As a counterbalance to this emotionally challenging exercise, it's helpful to make a gratitude list expressing what brings you contentment and peace in your life today.

_____

_____

_____

As you take stock of these losses, be sure to share them with a confidant. It's a bittersweet process to take a closer look at grief, loss, and regret. Consider reading the Acceptance Prayer from the *Alcoholics Anonymous: The Big Book* daily (you can also Google this prayer). Gratitude and acceptance will be your allies as you grieve the loss of the fantasy of how life was supposed to be.

## Closing Doors, Opening Doors

**Action Step:** One of the stickiest parts of grief tends to be regret. Name three primary regrets now.

_____

_____

_____

It's a heavy process to unearth regrets so don't forget to breathe, knowing that regrets are a portal to something new and different. For instance, one of my greatest regrets was not spending more time with my grandmother when she was aging. I was in Los Angeles during the last ten years of her life, and we spoke every Saturday morning, but I still feel loss as I write this to you. You see, I was "too busy" and "too broke" to travel to the east coast to see her more, yet I wasn't too busy to be on the hunt for sex. Despite that, I try to accept the fact that I was suffering at the time and did the best I knew how to do back then.

Regret may refer to something you didn't do, or it may refer to something you did that you wish you hadn't.

**Action Step:** For each regret identified, write an affirmation of self-compassion for the part of you that did the best you knew how. (For example, I did the best I knew how at the time.)

_____

_____

_____

In the twelve-step rooms, hitting bottom refers to the moment when you realize you need help and ask for it. If you chose to go to a twelve-step meeting, you probably found out quickly that you weren't alone with this problem. Even though hitting bottom can be excruciating, it's also a door to recovery and healing.

**Action Step:** When did you hit bottom? Describe the moment you knew you were *sick and tired of being sick and tired.*

_____

_____

_____

**Action Step:** What shifted within you once you admitted you needed help, and how have you been looking at ways to move forward into a more fulfilling life?

_____

_____

_____

The good news about grief is that it always brings new beginnings. Doors closing, doors opening. In my case, it allowed me to ask for help, to practice humility, to feel less alone and feel a sense of belonging with others in recovery, and eventually open up the aperture to consider what I really wanted out of life. Intimacy will always be a lifelong practice for me but I'm clear it's my neural pathway to feeling more comfortable in my own skin.

**Action Step:** What are your new beginnings? They may be bigger. They may be smaller but identify what is new in your life now that you have said goodbye to the losses.

_____

_____

_____

## Your Practice

1. Grief is part of being human, and it can be quite burdensome. Acknowledge, accept, and process your grief to make room for creative energy and possibilities.
2. It's not about letting go of the past as much as it's about learning to live with the past, no matter how complicated. You wouldn't be who you are if it wasn't for the past. Grieving allows you to live with the losses while unburdening the heaviness associated with it.
3. Fantasy is a big part of compulsive sexual behavior, but don't throw the baby out with the bathwater. Distinguish between healthier, liberating fantasy and obsessive, depleting forms of fantasy.
4. Swim with your dolphins—those people who are emotionally-dependable, fun, playful, and loyal. Say goodbye to anyone who doesn't meet these requirements.
5. Regrets are part of grief and therefore part of recovery. Embrace your regrets as an opportunity to forgive yourself and practice self-compassion.
6. On the other side of grief is resilience and resourcefulness. Give yourself plenty of time and space to grieve the losses and experience the resilient part of you.

## Reference

Campbell, Chellie. 2002. *The Wealthy Spirit: Daily Affirmations for Financial Stress Reduction.* Naperville, IL: Sourcebooks.

# 3 Turning Down the Volume on Shame

*Shame was palpable in my family. My parents were Depression-era babies who grew up in crowded one-bedroom apartments in Brooklyn, squeezing four people into each limited space. My father carried his version of shame throughout his life. It manifested in the idea that he didn't deserve the material things that he worked so hard to achieve. You wouldn't have detected it if you met him, but underneath his friendly exterior, he embodied a "not enough" way of being in the world. Although he played by the rules of his generation and advanced well beyond the simplicity of my grandparents' Eastern European origins, he lived a calculated, risk-avoidant life—an unconscious attempt to keep things small and safe, often a telltale sign of trauma and helplessness. The intergenerational hand-me-downs were undeniable as shame was pervasive in my childhood home. Instead of lifting each other up, we were too burdened by shame to even begin to engage in mutual encouragement.*

*Today shame lives inside of me as an insatiable hunger that still lingers. I don't find myself as ravenous as before and try my best to seek proper nutrition. Historically, my search to be fed stems from the myth that I was supposed to always be independent. It turns out that no five-year-old is supposed to be self-sufficient, yet I was rewarded for doing my own laundry and dragging the Hoover vacuum over our shag rugs. From a young age I was rewarded for "doing" rather than "being."*

*In retrospect, all I ever wanted was to be fully myself without apology. On some level I knew I was different from my three older brothers and the other boys in my neighborhood. I didn't understand it at the time as I tried to conform to typical boy activities, all the while knowing there was something different about me that I didn't understand at the time. Back in the 70s and 80s being gay was a big secret with a big stigma—fuel to the fire of shame.*

*By the spring of my sophomore year of college, in 1985, I couldn't hold back anymore, and I came out gradually to a few people I felt I could trust. My shame subsided little by little. But the carried shame of my parent's generation still lingered, and underneath it, I felt like I had to earn love rather than receive it unconditionally. I had a powerful need to be liked by others which resulted in me becoming an impeccable listener. My attunement to others became a gift and a wall for others to truly get to know me.*

*Over time I've learned that shame is simply a feeling that rolls in and out like the tide. Learning to receive unconditional love has been a powerful antidote even though I still unintentionally resist it. I try to avoid self-attack and try to be more resilient, so I don't have to follow the same shame spirals that my father experienced.*

DOI: 10.4324/9781032650487-4

*Most of all, I do my best to receive the love around me while practicing Mindful Self-Compassion, my primary ingredient for shame resilience.*

> **Action Step:** The experience of shame has been described as feeling unlovable and flawed. Therefore, do you feel unworthy of love and acceptance? Take a moment to write about any shame messages you were given by others or continue to inflict on yourself.

_____

_____

_____

Keep in mind the following shame elements.

- Shame is a universal emotion and gets instilled early in life.
- Sharing one's shame with others is terrifying and courageous.
- If you don't talk about shame, it grows and becomes more powerful.
- Shame and blame often go together.

Through her research, professor, author, and storyteller Brené Brown coined the term *shame resilience* which implies that shame doesn't fully go away but instead you learn to live with it and find ways to minimize its effects.

## Building Shame Resilience

Brown captures the trajectory moving from stubborn shame to shame resilience. She defines shame resilience as follows: a) capacity to recognize our experiences of shame b) ability to move through shame constructively, maintaining our authenticity and growing from our experiences and c) stronger, more meaningful connections with people in our lives. I would add that it's a shift in the nervous system toward buoyancy, resourcefulness, and regulation.

> **Action Step:** Without overthinking it, what is your shame story? As we move through this chapter, you may revise this story, but start with your family or a particular family member and focus on the idea of "not being good enough" and see what unfolds.

_____

_____

_____

Shame resilience also suggests the following action steps:

- Understanding your shame and recognizing what triggers you.

- Practicing reality checks with trusted confidants.
- Reaching out and sharing your shame story.

In other words, name the shame, talk about the shame, own your story, and tell your story.

Here is the distinction between guilt and shame. Guilt refers to your behavior, and shame refers to who you are.

- Guilt = I did something bad.
- Shame = I am bad.

## Shrinking the Shame: An Action Plan

Shame is a universal part of life and recovery, but that's not always a bad thing. Shame is one of our primary emotions, and it can be paralyzing and profoundly isolating if not explored and processed. It often shows up in the self-attacking language you sometimes use against yourself such as:

- I'm not good enough.
- I don't like myself.
- Something is wrong with me.
- My feelings are too big.

I've been leading therapy groups since 1992, and one of the greatest benefits of group therapy is shame reduction and feeling less isolated. My groups generally have eight people in them, and they are constantly giving each other honest feedback—sometimes warm and fuzzy, and at other times, very direct and not so easy to receive. What is apparent over time is that they build respect and trust for one another which often is a contrast to their families of origin.

**Action Step:** When you were growing up, were your feelings ignored or minimized? How often were you bullied or humiliated in school or in your neighborhoods?

_____

_____

_____


*Shame is given to us by others and shame is healed through others* (Brown). Shame messages start early and penetrate deeply.

Yet, healing is possible. For example, group therapy provides a reparative experience, and even group members with the deepest level of shame feel some relief as they realize they are not alone, and others truly care about them—sometimes a rare experience for those who go through life with the invisible suffering associated with shame.

Remember that there can also be healthy shame. Take the example of a recovering alcoholic who grew up in a family with little or no boundaries. As an adult, he talks loudly and doesn't listen to others. To understand that he creates distance from others, a close friend had to sit him down to let him know how he unintentionally pushes others away. To correct his behavior, he needed to feel some level of shame that became a catalyst for him to reset his boundaries—in this case how he built walls between himself and others.

**Action Step:**
Distinguish between healthier shame and carried shame. Remember that healthier shame lets you know if you've crossed boundaries or done something that is not in your integrity. On the other hand, carried shame usually stems from childhood messages that really don't belong to you. Track both versions of shame and write a few examples now.

_____

_____

_____

Don't forget to share your shame inventory with someone you trust. By breaking the secrecy, shame loses its power.

**Awareness Step:**
Your *inner critic* evolved from toxic shame, and when you fall into self-attack mode today, you're pouring salt into an old wound. John Bradshaw was one of the originators of the term *inner child* referring to the younger part of you that will always need nurturance, acceptance, and unconditional love. Through self-compassion and paying attention to your inner child, self-acceptance is possible. Twelve-step recovery describes *acceptance* as *the answer to all my problems today*, and acceptance is a daily practice.

**Action Step:**
Write a letter to your inner child and focus on full acceptance. Sometimes it's suggested to write the letter in your non-dominant hand to truly feel as if you are that little kid. Once you've completed the letter, share it with someone who accepts you fully.

_____

_____

_____

**Action Step:**
Shame is healed through others. Identify two to three people you trust and respect. Let them know that you want to build shame resilience and you need

their honest feedback. Ask them the following questions either in person (preferred method) or by phone: 1) What do you like about me? 2) How do you see me as a lovable person? Write down their responses and if they are loving and positive, savor them.

_____

_____

_____

## Action Step:

Judgment is part of being human, but if you feel you're being judged all the time, it fuels shame. Notice when you are judging others or when you are being judged by others. Develop boundaries with those who are judgmental of you. Track when you are being judgmental and know it's an old way to protect yourself. What purpose does judgment still serve? What are you protecting yourself from?

_____

_____

_____

## Action Step:

Perfectionism is a way to cope with shame and fear, but it also creates more pain and isolation. What are the payoffs of your perfectionism? Is it a preemptive strike so that nobody can get too close to you? Keep track of any perfectionistic tendencies and then write down how they relate to your shame.

_____

_____

_____

Once you name your survival strategies, they can no longer be blind spots. Instead, you'll catch them more quickly creating more resilience and acceptance of who you are today.

In closing, don't forget that shame is simply another emotion. It can be a stickier one than some of the others, but if you take steps to process it and share it with a dependable person, it will lose its power. By processing your shame, you'll clear out the unwanted, toxic waste and make room for self-compassion and imperfection.

## Stephanie's Story: Investigating Intergenerational Shame

*Stephanie was raised in a conservative Jewish home and was the granddaughter of Holocaust survivors. For those who may not be familiar with this type of family history,*

*there is often an abundance of guilt and shame stemming from the unfathomable tra-*
*gedies witnessed by those who were in the concentration camps. This is an example of*
*intergenerational trauma which I sometimes refer to as generational hand-me-downs.*

*In her home Stephanie's feelings were often minimized or dismissed. Shame was*
*palpable in her parents, and as their daughter, Stephanie absorbed some of the*
*suffering. Gratitude was emphasized: "Be grateful for what you have—we didn't*
*have anything." As a result, Stephanie believed that there was something wrong with*
*her and her family, leaving her with this shame story that was intractable.*

*Stephanie joined a therapy group in her late twenties after identifying her intimacy*
*blocks and her tendency to stay away from sex and love (sometimes referred to as*
*sexual or love anorexia). Little by little, she was able to accept some of the positive*
*reflections the group had to offer but Stephanie had built large walls of self-attack*
*that made it difficult for anything to stick. She stayed in the group for five years and*
*eventually was able to receive some of the love offered to her. It felt glacial to her, but*
*Stephanie now felt hope that sex and love might be worth exploring further outside*
*of the therapy room.*

## Stopping Self-Attack

Self-attack is often a preemptive strike. Before anyone else can inflict pain on you,
this survival strategy becomes a proactive attempt to protect yourself. As a result,
a wall of self-attack takes shape and keeps others from getting too close. It has
become a habit that is so automatic that you might not even notice it. In general, you learn to attack yourself when you've been attacked by others, whether
that be within the family or by an outside bully. Either way, you've absorbed the
idea that you're not a valuable human being, and this just isn't true. Shame and
self-attack are not viable options for self-compassion.

**Action Step:** Describe your relationship with self-attack.

_____

_____

_____

**Action Step:** What are you willing to do to reduce self-attack?

_____

_____

_____

## Uncovering Self-Compassion

As discussed, brokenheartedness is often the cause, and compulsive sexual
behavior is one of the effects. Of course, there is much more nuance to this

equation; however, healing the heartbreak requires self-compassion to ease the shame, hurt, self-loathing, and grief.

*I grew up in a family lacking compassion and self-compassion. I do believe there was buried love underneath it all along with lots of barriers preventing us from discovering safe enough connection. As a result, I was looking for love elsewhere— first with friends and their families and then with anonymous hookups. My efforts toward connection were well-intentioned but they were a misguided attempt toward authentic contact and intimacy.*

*My former associate, Jen, introduced me to Mindful Self-Compassion (MSC). In the past I heard about its growing popularity but never experienced an up close and personal account of it. Jen had returned from a retreat with Kristin Neff, one of the developers of MSC, which sparked a contagious enthusiasm in me. I remember a pivotal conversation when she suggested I listen to Chris Germer and Tara Brach, both talented self-compassion teachers, and I began listening to their guided meditations with fervor. Before I knew it, my morning MSC ritual evolved into one of my favorite daily tone setters. This morning practice resulted in the development of new neural pathways as well as shame reduction and self-compassion.*

Back in the 1990s I learned about the neuroplasticity of the brain—evidence that you can teach an old dog new tricks. My ingrained family patterns and sexual compulsivity were my well-worn paths that I lived with for the first few decades of my life. In my early thirties I added twelve-step meetings to my weekly therapy, and new pathways were being constructed including greater self-awareness, self-acceptance and self-compassion.

What exactly is Mindful Self-Compassion? Here are the three main components:

1. Self-kindness.
2. A sense of common humanity.
3. Mindfulness.

In *Self-Compassion Break*, Chris Germer's six-minute guided meditation, he walks the listener through these three steps. *Self-kindness* helps normalize your distress related to difficulties in your life and suggests you see this through the lens of compassion and patience. *Common humanity* refers to the fact that others are also going through similar challenges—you are not alone in your pain. *Mindfulness* reminds you that you can treat yourself in the same way you would treat a loved one. This practice reminds you that the healing of self is not an isolated moment, class, or workshop—it creates new neural pathways over time.

When you develop more compassion for yourself, you're also paving the way for greater self-acceptance as well as self-love. Deeper connection to self is a cornerstone of sustainable recovery as you find ways to turn down the volume on the inner critic and turn up the volume on healing.

**Action Steps:** How do you integrate these ideas into everyday living?

1. Decide if you're open to practicing self-compassion. Maybe you have other parts of your recovery you would like to address first. Do you have other life

priorities? Your choice to practice self-compassion is also about timing. Ask yourself if this is the best time for you to focus on this practice. Like everything, it takes time, energy, and investment. Determine if this is the right time for you.

2. Recite the following as a possible mantra "May I have the willingness to accept myself for exactly who I am at any given moment" and "May I have the willingness to accept _____ (fill in the blank with another person) for exactly who they are at any given moment." Acceptance and self-acceptance are close cousins of self-compassion.

3. Self-compassion and compassion are portable. Don't wait for a podcast or a book or even a prayer. Carry the intention of being more self-compassionate and eventually it will become part of your everyday being.

4. Consider group therapy.

Mindful Self-Compassion requires a conscious choice to be kinder to yourself. It sounds so easy, yet it's a lifelong practice. Identify the inner critic when it reveals itself and replace it with acceptance, patience, and compassion.

## Recovering from Perfectionism

*I was a child perfectionist. Not your average version of perfection, but a card-carrying, daily-practicing, CEO of childhood perfectionism. If I didn't understand instructions given to me by my Hebrew teacher, I would have a meltdown. If I didn't finish everything on my to-do list, I would go into a shame spiral. It was a painful version of trying to be perfect at all costs.*

*Because my home was full of chaos, competition, and shame, I found refuge in my bedroom and made attempts to keep things in meticulous order. Perfectionism helped me cope with my dysfunctional family, but often left me suffering when I couldn't achieve it—which was 100% of the time. The attempt to control things around me brought me misery, and I had to learn that perfectionism was a myth. Even though it gives the illusion of structure, it only provides temporary relief rather than sustainable healing.*

*Through years of therapy, twelve-step work and meditation, I've learned to take myself a bit less seriously. I aspire to be more lighthearted, and my perfectionism is not quite as heavy as it used to be. It still rears its ugly head when I'm under stress and when I forget to seek emotional nourishment. This may sound counterintuitive, but to stay on my healing path, I need to practice imperfection.*

*Recovery from out-of-control sexual behaviors is a long, winding road. Anyone who tells you otherwise is either lying or in denial. In the "beverage program" some people are able to put the plug in the jug and stay sober, but compulsive sex is another species, in which imperfection needs to be built into the healing process. Like food and money, sex needs to be integrated into one's life rather than practicing complete abstinence.*

## Janet's Story: Practicing Imperfection

*Janet had two years of time on her sexual recovery plan until she lost her job and unexpectedly needed to move out of the apartment she loved. The stress was too much, and she turned to her old ways of porn and masturbation as an attempt to cope with this double whammy. She attended two twelve-step meetings a week and worked on the steps weekly with her sponsor. Janet was no stranger to witnessing imperfections in the rooms, but this was her first personal experience of falling off the wagon. She told her sponsor what happened and was advised to go to a meeting ASAP and share about her recent stressors. As a result, she received a lot of encouragement to double up on her contact with program and to be compassionate with herself about the "slip." Initially, Janet felt shame, which slowly turned to relief when others revealed their imperfect, bumpy roads.*

As a recovering perfectionist, I thought that sexual recovery was going to be a linear progression. This wasn't my story, and it's not the story of many others. But I felt tremendous shame and fear if I couldn't adhere firmly to my plan. Unfortunately, I still see profound shame and loneliness in newcomers who face early difficulties.

The final chapter in my book, *It's Not About the Sex*, is entitled "It's Not the Mistakes That Count," and illustrates and celebrates imperfection. I believe that stumbling and fumbling is a growth opportunity unlike any other. Rather than falling into a shame spiral of despair and isolation, it can truly be an opportunity for curiosity, self-observation, and non-judgment. Perfectionism is a setup for brokenheartedness.

Recovery from compulsive sex can be a road full of detours, and embracing a paradigm shift of imperfection presents a growth opportunity not often discussed. Practicing imperfection requires a mindful approach toward implementing sustainable healing strategies even when things go off course. Try not to follow these ideas too perfectly, but instead, consider which ones would be realistic for you to practice on a regular basis.

**Action Step**: Normalize imperfection as a necessary part of your recovery. Look at detours as a learning opportunity. Begin with two columns. In the first column, take a daily inventory of what you have identified as your imperfections. In the second column, write down what you can learn from each of them. Keep track for twenty-one days.

_____

_____

_____

**Action Step:** Celebrate your imperfections. Refer to your "imperfection inventory" and write about your gratitude for the less-than-perfect parts of you.

_____

_____

_____

**Action Step:** Practice shame resilience. Brené Brown has studied the growth potential connected to shame resilience. Write about a memory when you noticed your shame resilience.

_____

_____

_____

Mindful Self-Compassion is another antidote to perfectionism. There are three parts to this practice: 1. Identify something or someone in your life that is causing you distress. 2. Know that you are part of the human condition and others all around the world have similar distress. 3. Try to be as compassionate to yourself as you would be for a loved one.

**Action Step:** What does Mindful Self-Compassion mean to you? Describe a recent experience when you practiced self-compassion or might have utilized this simple but powerful method.

_____

_____

_____

Perfectionism isolates you because you feel alone in your suffering. Connect with your therapist, coach, sponsor, loved one, and/or higher power. By establishing deeper contact with others, you will feel less alone and less anxious.

**Action Step:** Who will you contact when you are suffering from your perfectionism?
   Work toward regulating your nervous system on a regular basis. Dysregulation is part of being human, and perfectionism fuels dysregulation as anxiety and fear grow underneath.

_____

_____

_____

Consider talking to a somatically trained professional to help you build somatic awareness and feel embodied more of the time.

## Your Practice

1. You are worthy of unconditional love and acceptance. If you already feel this, notice what it's like to feel lovable. If not, hold this bigger intention as a possibility of longer-term healing.
2. Listen to your broken record of shame messages. Notice them with curiosity and nonjudgment to try and understand what purpose this may serve.
3. Build shame resilience. Because shame is a natural emotion that is part of being human, choose to efficiently process the shame.
4. Shame is an emotion, and self-attack is a punitive action. Notice when you slide into self-attack and stop this habit.
5. Healthy shame lets you know when you have crossed boundaries-either those within yourself or with others. Pay attention to times when this happens and re-calibrate more effective boundaries.
6. Self-compassion and compassion from others are antidotes to chronic shame attacks. Practice compassion for yourself and others.
7. Judgment, blame, and perfectionism are all neighbors in the shame neighborhood. Observe and minimize these tendencies and ask yourself how they related to shame.

## References

Brown, Brené. 2010. *The Gifts of Imperfection: Let Go of Who You Think You're Supposed to Be and Embrace Who You Are*. Center City, MN: Hazelden.

Germer, Christopher. 2019. *Self-Compassion Break*. https://youtu.be/T_80y_CT32c..tps://youtu.be/T_80y_CT32c

Bradshaw, John. 1990. *Healing the Shame that Binds You*. Deerfield Beach, FL: Health Communications, Inc.

# 4 Moving Beyond Narcissism

*I used to think the world revolved around me. As the golden child of the family, it always seemed like I would get my way no matter what. Maybe this was an early version of healthy entitlement—the belief that if I wanted it enough, it would eventually come to me. Or maybe it was my make-believe bubble that I could always get what I want if I whined long enough to get it. Yet, I realized early on that I had been born into a troubled family and held on to the belief that my narcissistic wall would protect me from the unpredictable storms that inevitably came my way in my family. Somehow, I held on to the fantasy that my family was functional, but it became clear that this was just an illusion.*

*Although she tried to raise four boys, my mother's capacity to keep up with all her roles and responsibilities was rather limited. Don't get me wrong. My mom did the best she knew how with a strong veneer of narcissism that left me longing for some kind of meaningful contact. Maybe she modeled for me how narcissism can be a way of regulating the distance from others in order to keep people at a safe distance.*

*Nowadays it seems that a narcissistic personality is often seen as some kind of plague, but let's face it, we all have a narcissistic layer within us. I believe my narcissism has given me the courage and the ambition to stretch beyond my so-called comfort zone and move toward a bigger life. In contrast to my mother and several others in my family, I've chosen a profession where I get to practice empathy skills and attunement. Although I've had these skills from early on, developing empathy with all humans (and animals) is one of the antidotes to narcissism. Whenever a client puts their trust in me, it feels like a sacred agreement as I devote my calling to healing, growing, and deepening—both in my clients and in myself. Now I get to break the family legacy.*

Beneath narcissism is brokenheartedness. Although it may not be evident at first, early heartbreak is often the birthplace of narcissistic tendencies. Narcissism is generally seen as a negative trait, but in this chapter, I choose to see it as neither positive nor negative, but instead a part of all of us worthy of deeper understanding. When babies are born, they imagine that the world revolves around them, a natural response to moving from being in utero to exploring the world. If they have an immediate need (food, touch, change of diaper), they hold the belief that someone will take care of their needs efficiently. Unfortunately, the fantasy that your caregiver will respond to you in just the right way, at just the right time, at just the right temperature, sets you up for the first of many narcissistic injuries to come. And every one of you will suffer from narcissistic wounds

DOI: 10.4324/9781032650487-5

throughout the course of your lifetime. It's not the wounds that count. It's how you deal with them.

As you know quite well, there are no guarantees in childhood. As a matter of fact, you didn't get what you wanted exactly when you wanted it—one definition of entitlement—and one of the hallmarks of narcissism. Most of you learn to cope with the challenges and unpredictability of relationships and adapt accordingly. True narcissists do not. They hold on stubbornly to their idea of entitlement and have a stubborn lack of empathy for others. On the other hand, healthy narcissism refers to the intrinsic belief that you are desirable, lovable human beings and others can be trusted over time. The story of Charlie illustrates the healthier side of narcissism.

### Charlie's Story: Recognizing the Healthier Side of Narcissism

*Having grown up in a loveless home with depressed parents and four older, distant siblings, Charlie was profoundly lonely. As the fifth child, he always felt like he raised himself as he learned to take care of chores, such as polishing the furniture by the time he was in first grade. His level of self-sufficiency was way beyond his years.*

*Because he was a pleasant surprise," he was considerably younger than his siblings. As a result, he felt separate and superior at times. He was even placed in a program for kids who excelled academically, which set him apart even further and perpetuated the aura of specialness which fed Charlie's version of narcissism.*

*Having grown up in a home with intense criticism, high emphasis on achievement, and a string of infidelities by both parents, perfectionism became Charlies' way of getting validation and attention. Although he was very isolated, Charlie's healthier form of narcissism helped him feel competent amid constant competition, envy, and bullying.*

Here are some practical steps to consider:

**Action Step**: Describe your understanding as to the differences between healthier narcissism and harmful narcissism.

_____

_____

_____

Healthier narcissism will generally show up when you're feeling more emotionally resilient, confident, and connected to others. Harmful forms of narcissism show up as chronic relationship problems, blaming others, and lack of empathy or attunement. Because we all possess each of these qualities, track which qualities are more prevalent and focus your attention on what you aspire to.

**Action step:** Addictive, compulsive behaviors are narcissistic by nature, often leaving you in a bubble, segregated from others. How can you bring self-compassion to the narcissistic part of yourself by recognizing it as a universal part of the human condition?

_____

_____

_____

We all have a different version of it—some more extreme and some more subtle. Give yourself a break and learn about narcissism as part of you—not something that defines you.

## Practicing Other-Centeredness

We live in a "me-first" culture. Putting others first is a practice, especially if you're not used to it. We get mixed messages in our culture. Follow your bliss. Ask yourself what you really want. Determine your highest priorities. Let me be clear: I'm not suggesting you focus on others at your own expense. That would be another chapter devoted to codependency.

Instead, create a balanced focus between others and yourself. The Prayer of Saint Francis suggests we love before being loved, we pardon before being pardoned, etc. I hear wisdom in these words. Keep in mind that your capacity to give is immense.

**Action Step:** Name the ways that you are now giving to others in your life.

_____

_____

_____

**Action Step:** As you specify ways in which you are generous, how would you like to build on that part of you?

_____

_____

_____

Although my grandmother was the embodiment of generosity, she probably leaned in the direction of being selfless and what we might label as codependent today. She was a dutiful mother, wife, and grandmother, which can be a beautiful thing, or it may have left her too "other-centered." This seemed to be her identity, so if I was able to ask her about this today, she might not be able to fully grasp this idea of balance. Yet, her version of other-centeredness seemed to give her life meaning within the family. And I am forever grateful for her ability to give fully and unconditionally from her heart. The gift of a lifetime for me.

**Action Step:** What is the difference between self-centeredness and other-centeredness?

_____

_____

_____

Observe when you tend to be more giving and when you are hungrier to receive. How would you like to practice other-centeredness? By giving back (or being of service) you will feel more of a sense of belonging.

_____

_____

_____

**Action Step:** Be of service. Consider volunteering, which comes in many shapes and forms. For instance, you have friends who can't afford a dog sitter for the weekend. Volunteer to look after their dog, which can be helpful to them but also an exercise in receiving unconditional love from this furry friend.

**Action Step:** Full-blown narcissism and open-hearted love cannot coexist. If you find yourself reading this chapter and getting in touch with a level of loneliness, start small. Would you like to consider adopting a pet or possibly planting a home garden?

_____

_____

_____

Who are the emotionally dependable people in your life?

_____

_____

_____

The opposite of narcissism is empathy, unconditional generosity, and deeper connection.

**Action Step:** Cultivate your generosity of spirit. What are a few ways you can give back to others who have given so much to you?

_____

_____

_____

Hold the door open for someone. Donate to your favorite charity. Be respectful of others in all walks of life. A simple way of giving is to say hello or smile at your neighbors.

**Action Step:** Entitlement and envy are ways of protecting yourself from being hurt. Name a recent experience when you had feelings of entitlement (or envy).

_____

_____

_____

Now name a way to take responsibility for those feelings. For instance, if you are feeling entitled to something right away, practice patience. If you notice envy, try to be happy for the person you envy rather than falling into competition with them.

**Action Step:** As human beings, we all experience narcissistic ruptures along the way. Depending on the extent of your past wounds, intimacy will be a challenge. Begin to notice when you are feeling vulnerable. Go slow. Pace yourself and try to take bite-size emotional risks. What kind of small risk are you willing to take with someone you trust?

_____

_____

_____

As a result, you'll create more of an authentic connection in your relationships. Consider joining a therapy group which is one of the best ways to build relationship muscle and to practice vulnerability in a safer, more productive way.

In summary, narcissism is a self-protective survival strategy and it's not always a bad thing. It's only problematic when someone is unwilling to look at patterns that get in their way. We all have a narcissistic layer inside of us which can present a challenge and an opportunity to learn about ourselves more deeply. Observe yourself with curiosity and nonjudgment and see what you discover.

## Awakening Generosity

Narcissism mutes your generosity. Part of being human is a desire for connection, and one of the primary ways to connect is through giving as well as receiving. Yet, this may be a vulnerable thing to do if you're not used to it because it ultimately introduces intimacy.

**Action Step**: How do you see yourself being compassionate to others? It may be to other humans or possibly to your pet.

_____

_____

_____

**Action Step:** When do you put yourself in the shoes of others? This is one description of empathy which is a tool toward healing narcissism.

_____

_____

_____

**Action Step**: How do you give back to your community, family, workplace, etc.?

_____

_____

_____

## Exploring Longing and Belonging

*We are most defended against our greatest needs.* Borrowed from a psychoanalytic perspective, this phrase carries a lot of wisdom, so let's break it down. We are all born with a longing for belonging, and then the reality of our family, community, and schools comes along and it's not so simple. In your heart of hearts, feeling a part of something greater than yourself is just the nourishment you hunger for. Sometimes it's more available and sometimes not so much. When a profound loneliness sets in at times, it's likely that you will retreat and build walls against intimacy. In other words, you will become protected against your deep desire for connection and love. This is the human condition. When a child does not receive unconditional love and acceptance, the wall of narcissism generally grows.

**Action Step:** Write about a childhood experience when you really wanted to belong, but you were rejected.

_____

_____

_____

**Action Step:** Write about a more recent experience when you wanted to belong to a group, and you felt acceptance.

_____

_____

_____

Longing for a sense of belonging is emotionally risky because you never know what you're going to get in return. Without taking the risk, you will never know. Yes, it can be quite scary, but wearing your heart on your sleeve is the only avenue toward deeper contact with others. Belonging requires a willingness to be humble and ask for acceptance. Sometimes you will be invited to join and other times you may be excluded. This is not a reflection on you. The victory is in the risk-taking, and it's the only way to find out.

## Your Practice

1. Be aware of narcissistic tendencies in yourself and in others. Observe what's below the surface—possibly deeper longings, fears, loneliness. Be compassionate for these human parts which often show up as traits of selfishness, self-centeredness, and distancing.
2. Scratch the surface of compulsive sexual behavior and you'll find a narcissistic underbelly. It's inside all of us—those in recovery and those not in recovery. Observe your version of narcissism.
3. *Being of service* is recommended in all twelve-step fellowships because you move from self-centeredness to other-centeredness. Getting out of your own head can bring relief and perspective so track your efforts toward other-centeredness.
4. Entitlement can be defined as *wanting what you want when you want it.* Sounds like a toddler throwing a tantrum, but we all do this at one time or another. Catch your entitlement moments when they happen and investigate how it still functions in your life.
5. Narcissistic injury happens when something doesn't go your way and bruises your ego. Injury is inevitable but repair is where the real work begins. Once you identify the injury, find a confidant to work toward mending this wound.
6. Narcissism acts as a wall—a protective way to keep people at a distance. The longer-term healing is to build trust and intimacy safely and gradually. Hold this intention even if it doesn't feel safe enough today.

# 5 Regulating the Nervous System

*Having grown up in the 70s in a turbulent family, I found creative ways to cope with the chaos of our home. First, I worked hard to find best friends in my neighborhood. As a matter of fact, I was lucky enough to be adopted by three families before the age of fourteen. I also tried to stay as busy as possible. Except for stopping long enough to watch the 70s sitcoms such as* All in the Family *and* M.A.S.H., *I was always on the go. Doing, achieving, and perfecting became my survival strategies to avoid the sadness, hurt, and anger deep within. If I did enough, achieved enough, and perfected enough, somehow, I would be more lovable and desirable. These coping skills worked well enough until they stopped working in high school.*

*Although I was rather resilient and resourceful, my survival strategies left me longing for unconditional love from my family. Instead, I experienced competition, envy, and shame. As a result, my perfectionism grew intolerable. All I really wanted was to be loved for who I was—a curious kid, longing for authentic connection. In retrospect, I realize that I was doing the best I knew how, but my way of distancing mushroomed into out-of-control sexual behaviors.*

*In the early 90s I had a very wise therapist named Burt, who strongly suggested I slow down and listen to the "rhythm within," or my underlying misery would grow. At the time, I had never heard this expression and it deeply resonated with me because I had always been so compulsively busy as to ignore what was really going on inside of me. He was the first person who ever told me that I needed to throw away my "to-do lists" to make room for simply being.*

*More than a quarter of a century later, I admit that I am still a list-maker but I'm not doing it compulsively or unconsciously. In addition to my other compulsive tendencies, perfectionism and "busy-ness" pre-dated some of my other vices. In some ways they were the birthplace of my attempts to numb and feel less.*

## Following the Rhythm Within

For those of you who attend twelve-step meetings or may be interested in considering them, listening to the rhythm within goes hand in hand with a first step and an eleventh step. By admitting you have a problem, you've already slowed down long enough to observe your suffering. You made a mindful choice to ask for help and look for others whose lives had improved. One day at a time you might establish a connection with a power greater than yourself—and you might call this power God, Universal Power, or Higher Power. Possibly Nature

DOI: 10.4324/9781032650487-6

or beloved pets are a starting gate for a power greater than yourself, and pets have always been a touchstone of fun, laughter, and connection in my life. By looking within, you will start to examine what matters most to you.

**Action Step:** Do you believe in a Higher Power? If so, describe this entity. If not, describe what keeps you from believing in this possibility.

_____

_____

_____

Once the out-of-control sexual behaviors quiet down, there is now space inside of you to practice the art of relaxation. Most of us design barriers to keep us from truly relaxing. It's not just vegging in front of the TV or surfing the internet. Instead, it's a physiological winding down which only happens when we mind-fully carve out a space for our nervous system to *rest and digest*.

**Action Step:** How do you relax?

_____

_____

_____

Because American culture rewards busy-ness and accomplishment, relaxation is the road less traveled. Mindful recovery takes place when we break away from the routine and regulate the nervous system, possibly through somatic exercises related to grounding, orienting, and resourcing, just to name a few.

Early in my career I asked my clients to identify their thoughts and feelings. In the early 1990s this was the norm for most psychotherapists—a traditional approach to learning about the clinical themes and patterns of the past and how they influence the here and now. What I've learned through the years is that insight and awareness can be therapeutic, but trauma healing also requires attention to the connection between brain and body.

*Because of the distress I endured as a kid, I built a fortress of walls that I still climb. What I've come to understand is that I needed to avoid the danger I experienced in my home. I learned how to navigate the suffering by living in my head and ignoring the anguish stored in my body. I also learned how to be self-sufficient, avoiding the disappointment of others letting me down.*

*Seeking sex became my attempt to feel better. As a result, I felt numb and disconnected at times, yet sometimes I felt adrenaline and excitement. Was I looking for love in all the wrong places? Maybe, but I was also learning about myself—exploring, experimenting, investigating. Sometimes I felt more alive as a result of my sexual adventures. All I knew at the time was that I wanted to feel something other than profound isolation. Today I'm truly grateful for the period in my life when I was constantly on the hunt for sex, validation, and attention. It turned out to be the greatest wake-up call to restore my nervous system.*

*Three decades later I've learned that my body is the most accurate barometer of what's happening inside of me and can help bring me into alignment: mind, body, and spirit. Now I understand that chronic dysregulation in my nervous system left me highly vulnerable to chronic compulsive behaviors. I need to check in daily if not more than once daily to see if I'm feeling comfortable in my skin or not. If not, I now have a toolbox of possibilities to return to a more regulated, resilient state more effectively. And that's what we're going to explore in this chapter.*

As I mentioned, Burt was a one-of-a-kind mentor. By the time we met, he was already in his seventies, and I was in my late twenties. Upon meeting, it was clear that he had a non-traditional clinical toolbox that went back to the 1960s. Before a session he asked me to wait in his living room which looked out into his backyard, which was a tropical wonderland. Burt converted his garage into his office with an eclectic décor of masks from around the world and beanbag chairs all around the space. I knew from the beginning that he was going to challenge me in a way I never knew before. This unusual therapeutic relationship turned out to be one of my first regulating relationships.

**Action Step:** Who has been most influential in your life? A sponsor, teacher, therapist, coach? List them here.

_____

_____

_____

**Action Step:** What was significant about this person (s)? How did they change the course of your life?

_____

_____

_____

Cultivating relationships with emotionally reliable people regulates your nervous system. Whether it's a mentor or another dependable person in your life, trusting others is a pillar of recovery both from compulsive behaviors and trauma. If you were unable to identify any mentors, don't give up. Keep your eyes and ears open for "your people." Someone influential is bound to cross your path if you stay open-hearted to the possibility.

One of the themes of my work with Burt was to become more familiar with my internal world. He helped me see that my mind always seemed to be on the go, and it was preventing me from fully connecting with him. Intuitively, I knew that my busy mind was creating a distance from others and preventing me from experiencing the intimacy I longed for, but Burt was the first person to spell this out for me and reflect this obvious but profound intimacy barrier. By the time I met him, I was winding down my daily habits with compulsive sexual behavior. As we discussed in Chapter One, sexual sobriety doesn't equate to emotional resilience, and my mind was still working overtime.

**Action Step:** How does your busy-ness keep you at an emotional distance from others?

_____

_____

_____

**Action Step:** How has this been a way of protecting yourself?

_____

_____

_____

How does this relate to the nervous system? A busy mind also refers to an anxious mind. Whether its high anxiety resulting in panic attacks or generalized anxiety that seems to be an undercurrent most of the time, these are forms of dysregulation. One way of reducing vulnerability to compulsive behavior is moving toward a regulated nervous system. So how do you slow down and regulate?

**Action Step**: Reflect on times when you were able to quiet the mind as a child. Recall any specific memories. List these "slowdown" moments now.

_____

_____

_____

**Action Step:** Your way of slowing down as a kid may be a clue to strategies as a grown-up. How do you want to practice slowing down from now on?

_____

_____

_____

*Rest and relaxation are a lost art. When I was a kid, I had a best friend named Danny who was always available to simply hang out. I would call him on my red rotary phone and ask, "What are you doing?" and he would typically answer,*

"Nothing." So, I would respond, "Wanna do nothing together?" and he would always enthusiastically say, "Absolutely. Let's do nothing together!"

Not only was this a true sign of friendship, but it was also an opportunity to discover our next adventure and sometimes plan very little. I don't know about you, but I don't really have friends like that anymore, but the principle remains the same. How do I hang out with myself (or with others) and practice R&R in a quality way on a regular basis?

Recently, I spent time with my family of choice in the San Juan Islands just north of Seattle. It's become a summer retreat where I get to do nothing for a week. As a matter of fact, I work hard to do as little as possible. Because I tend to be a to-do list kind of guy, it takes mindful effort to decompress and truly relax. And this has become an integral part of the rhythm of my yearly calendar not unlike my childhood days "doing nothing together."

I don't see these retreats as optional anymore. They help me push the reset button. I know this goes against the Puritanical work ethic many of us learned, but unwinding and decompressing is a vital part of my work, which gives me the capacity to be more present and more refreshed when I return to the office.

In the rooms of Sex and Love Addicts Anonymous, they refer to top-line behaviors as anything that feeds the soul and enriches your recovery. It's not just an exercise to develop a list of possibilities, but a mandate to start practicing them on a consistent basis.

For example, one of the top-line behaviors I regularly practice is daily meditation. For many years I dabbled in meditation but never found traction with an ongoing practice. What finally worked for me was signing up for a Mindfulness Meditation class with a focus on stress reduction (aka MBSR). And this class provided structure and accountability as well as the motivation of a financial investment. All these things worked well for me, and after a few months of practice while having a teacher encouraging me, it finally stuck.

My morning ritual is simple. I sit quietly on my cushion in a designated space in my home. Then I read one page from an inspirational book as well as a morning prayer that resonates with me. I then sit for ten minutes. As a recovering perfectionist, I try not to beat myself up for not sitting longer, but instead I try and honor myself for the time I do commit to sitting.

This is the tone setter for my day. I feel the difference when I skip my morning ritual, and my day tends to flow easier when I engage in this sacred morning space. For me, mindful meditation is one way to regulate my nervous system and to breathe into the knowledge that I'm simply a living, breathing organism just like all the other human beings on our planet.

I forgot to mention that my cocker spaniel, Bowie, sits (or sleeps) in the room with me as he patiently waits for our morning walk, and his presence is also quite regulating for me and my nervous system. Whether you find ways of self-regulating or mutually regulating, your system relaxes when you feel more trusting in yourself, others, and your environment.

These are simply a few tips to unwind, decompress and push the re-set button. It's taken me a long time to get to the point where I truly prioritize R&R, but *now I know it's a requirement to live the life I choose to live. You may stumble and fumble along the way but give yourself the space for rest and relaxation and see what happens.*

Slowing down takes different shapes and forms, but the goal is to decelerate, live in the present moment and reduce the burden of anxiety you carry. Recently, my therapist, Jesse suggested that I end my day by reading something inspirational. In the past, I watched a rerun of *Seinfeld* or *Modern Family* to unwind. Not that there is anything wrong with TV time in moderation, but I was curious about his suggestion. Now I keep a biography or an inspirational book by my night table and try to keep my eyes open to read just a few pages before turning off the light. This is a bookend to my morning tone setter, and I believe it's also helped me sleep more restfully.

**Action Step:** What are you willing to do differently to bookend your day? What would you like your morning practice to be? What would you like your evening bedtime ritual to be?

_____

_____

_____

## Endorsing Rest and Relaxation

We all know that relaxation is a necessary part of life. I would go as far to say that R&R and taking time off work is a necessary part of our work. To show up fully for our professional life, we need to find balance. In American culture it's often encouraged to work long hours and take limited vacation time. This is not practiced in many other countries and continents because there is a core value on balance and family. Without down time, there is a vulnerability to more addictive, compulsive behaviors.

**Action Step**: What does rest and relaxation mean to you?

_____

_____

_____

**Action Step**: What are your current ways of relaxing?

_____

_____

_____

**Action Step:** Name additional ways you might consider relaxing?

_____

_____

_____

**Action Step:** How much time off do you take each year?

_____

_____

_____

**Action Step:** How much time off would you like to take each year? This might be an aspiration for now but ask yourself honestly how much time that might take.

_____

_____

_____

When it comes to slowing down and listening more intently to the rhythm within, there is no one size fits all. It will take some trial and error to see what works best for you. My cocker spaniel mix, Bowie, always fits into this conversation. Dogs are mindfulness teachers because they live solely in the present tense. He offers unconditional love and just wants to be touched, walked, and given treats in return. Not too different from us, right? Bowie knows when he needs to sleep and curls up in his bed very contently when he chooses to wind down.

**Action Step**: Who are your mindfulness teachers?

_____

_____

_____

Of course, he doesn't have the same responsibilities or schedule that we do, but he instinctively listens to his natural rhythm and rests when his body tells him to rest and plays when he wants connection.

Awareness Step: Listen to your body and see what it must tell you.

Bowie also brings out the inner child in me. In my childhood I had a Siberian husky for eleven years until I left for college, and then I went without a dog for more than two decades. When our first cocker spaniel, Cooper, arrived, he awakened a part of me that had been dormant. I immediately fell into the here and now experience of being with this little creature, and as a result, he became my mindfulness teacher. Nowadays, if I am mindful of our connection, we mutually regulate our nervous systems and help each other relax and feel safe.

_____

_____

_____

**Action Step:** When do you feel most calm and peaceful? Take a moment to savor it.

_____

_____

_____

Start your day with a mindful tone setter you enjoy. After my meditation, I mindfully stretch each morning and give gratitude to my back especially when it's pain-free. Back pain seems to be genetic in my family and I try to pay extra attention to it through daily stretching and yoga and outdoor swimming. Choose your version of a tone setter. You can do just about anything that creates a peaceful tone for your day.

**Action Step:** What would be a fun, satisfying morning tone setter?

_____

_____

_____

Hold mindfulness as a daily intention. At the beginning of my MBSR class, the teacher asked us to hold a raisin in our hand and simply look at it. She then instructed us to place it on our tongue without eating it—just noticing the texture. We then chewed it extra slowly to notice the skin and the juicy nature of it. Finally, we swallowed the raisin and noticed it going down our throat and imagining it make its way to our stomach and nourishing us. The raisin exercise was very impactful as it symbolized the automatic pilot that we inhabit most of the time. Pay attention and focus on your eating, walking, talking, physical contact, etc. Mindfulness is a powerful tool to observe yourself in the moment. Sometimes it may feel pleasant and sometimes not so pleasant.

**Awareness Step:** Observe yourself and track a few moments without judgment.

By listening carefully, there will be more of you to connect with others. A wise chaplain once called this the ministry of presence. When you are with loved ones, colleagues, pets, neighbors, you don't have to do anything. Being yourself is enough.

_____

_____

_____

**Action Step:** Identify a time in your past when you practiced the ministry of presence (more than likely without knowing it).

_____

_____

_____

**Awareness step:** Instead of being lost in the distractions of busy-ness, list making, or compulsive activities, see what it's like to simply be you. Sounds so simple, yet it's one of the most challenging aspects of daily life. Remember that there is no right or wrong, and no good or bad. This is truly an opportunity to build capacity for the resourceful, regulated part of you and in turn, to share this with others in your life.

_____

_____

_____

We are born into this world with resilience, resourcefulness, and regulation. Unfortunately, various types of traumas come along and tamper with those innate qualities. As a result, children discover other ways of coping and self-soothing. This may lead to compulsive tendencies. Keep in mind that compulsions serve a purpose and are survival strategies. You were doing the best you knew how.

**Action Step:** What purpose did your sexual compulsivity serve at one time?

_____

_____

_____

Every child needs unconditional love and acceptance to thrive, and many of us experienced emotional gaps in our families. My compulsive tendencies appeared first through perfectionism and order. For example, I used to line up my toys against the wall and kept them highly organized—not a typical trait for a seven-year-old.

**Action Step:** What were your earliest compulsive tendencies?

_____

_____

_____

**Action Step:** How were these compulsions forms of survival?

_____

_____

_____

## Opening the Window of Resilience

Elaine Miller-Karas, LCSW, executive director of the Trauma Resource Institute here in Southern California, developed the following diagram to illustrate regulation and dysregulation in the nervous system.

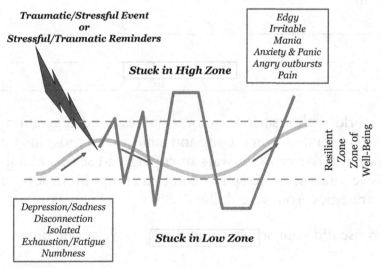

Graphic adapted by Elaine Miller-Karas, LCSW, Trauma. Resource Institute.

The space between the two dotted lines illustrates when you're feeling most resilient and buoyant (aka Window of Resilience). In other words, when you feel most like yourself. When you bump out of the resilience zone due to past trauma or life's stressors, you're vulnerable to feeling up-regulated or down-regulated. This generally happens when something feels like too much to process at the time.

When you "up-regulate," it feels like the accelerator inside you is revving high. This can manifest in things like panic attacks or rage. If your nervous system "down regulates," it feels like the brakes inside you are on. As a result, you might feel disconnected, depressed, or dissociated. Dysregulation is part of being human, and finding your way back to a regulated state is a challenge and opportunity.

Because chronic dysregulation can lead to syndromes like migraines, irritable bowel syndrome, and fibromyalgia, learning how to regulate more efficiently is essential for trauma healing as well as vulnerability to compulsive behaviors.

**Action Step:** Identify your typical most likely forms of dysregulation.

_____

_____

_____

## Examining Regulation, Dysregulation, and Attachment

Reliable caregivers help infants regulate their nervous systems, and attachment patterns originate in the connection between a baby and its caregiver. Unfortunately, many of you did not have emotionally dependable parents, leaving you at risk of compulsive behaviors.

**Action Step:** Name the emotionally dependable people in your childhood.

_____

_____

_____

**Action Step:** Name the emotionally dependable people in your adulthood.

_____

_____

_____

If you had a secure attachment with your caregiver, you're able to regulate your nervous system more easily and show more resilience. But if you had an insecure attachment, self-regulation becomes more challenging in childhood, as well as in later life. I believe that we can all identify with these patterns. I used to believe that my role as therapist was to help my clients establish a secure attachment. There may be some truth in that, but the primary goal is to break down the barriers clients may have built against secure attachment.

**Action Step:** What are your barriers to secure attachment?

_____

_____

_____

Although there are four major categories in the attachment literature, the two most common styles among sexual compulsives are Avoidant Attachment and Anxious Attachment. The other two categories are Secure Attachment and Disorganized Attachment. Secure attachment occurs when there is a *good-enough* parent, and children with addictive, compulsive patterns don't fall into this category.

## Avoidant Attachment

When a primary caregiver lacks the capacity to respond effectively to your needs, you experience them as emotionally unreliable. You become super self-sufficient, or "need-less and want-less," as Pia Mellody describes it. The mis-attuned parent creates a child who likewise denies needing support from others and has an *avoidant attachment*. This is the birthplace of love avoidance (sometimes called intimacy avoidance). Individuals learn to build relational walls to prevent feeling disappointed or overwhelmed.

**Action Step:** Do you identify with an avoidant attachment style? If so, describe how it shows up.

_____

_____

_____

## Anxious Attachment

When a primary caregiver is responsive and nurturing on some occasions, yet intrusive and insensitive at others, you're left anxious, insecure, and sometimes ambivalent, not knowing which version of the parent will show up at any given moment. You walk on eggshells and become highly distrustful, all the while feeling starved for contact. This type of inconsistent attunement results in an *anxious attachment*.

This is how love addiction and obsessive fantasy originate. To regulate the nervous system, the child seeks some type of soothing from the caregiver but never knows when, or if, it will come. As a result, the child is often desperate for contact and love that are only intermittently available.

**Action Step:** Do you identify with an anxious attachment style? If so, describe how this manifests.

_____

_____

_____

Just because there were attachment gaps in your past doesn't mean you're destined to remain avoidant, ambivalent, or anxious about relationships. Discovering and cultivating emotionally reliable relationships will keep the healing rolling.

**Action Step:** Who are the most emotionally dependable people in your life?

_____

_____

_____

**Awareness Step:** Notice when you relax around someone you trust. Your nervous system will let you know if you feel relaxed, calm, and safe enough with the other person.

_____

_____

_____

**Action Step:** When was the last time you felt most like yourself? For me, singing, laughing, and being silly with my dog is when I feel most like myself.

_____

_____

_____

**Action Step:** Which activities allow you to feel comfortable in your own skin?

_____

_____

_____

**Nervous System Glossary**

**Action Step:** Familiarize yourself with the language of the nervous system:

1. *Grounding:* an awareness of your body's physical contact with the background or something else that stabilizes it such as a supportive chair. Ground yourself anytime you feel dysregulated.
2. *Orienting:* giving your attention to the environment around you; you notice your surroundings and let your eyes go wherever they want to go. Orient yourself whenever you feel dissociated or disconnected.
3. *Pendulation:* the natural swing in the nervous system between pain or discomfort and sensations that are neutral or pleasant. Pay attention to the natural waves of your nervous system.
4. *Resilience Zone:* When you feel most regulated and more whole in mind, body, and spirit—sometimes called "being in flow." Savor times of resilience by letting yourself take note of these calm, peaceful, internal experiences.
5. *Resource:* A positive characteristic, a pleasant memory, a person, place, animal, or thing that provides a peaceful inner sensation. Use resourcing anytime you feel dysregulated.
6. *Titration:* Gradual exposure to sensations of distress, discomfort, or pain to prevent overwhelming your nervous system. Be patient and gentle with trauma healing. You always get to choose how much or how little you delve into it.
7. *Tracking sensations:* Pay attention to your physical sensations. By tracking, you'll move away from being a talking head and experience more connection to your brain and your body.

**Your Practice**

1. Describe your relationship with a *Higher Power.* You may be comfortable with the word God, Universal Energy, Nature, or your favorite pet. Anyone who is fully in your corner. If you don't relate to any of these possibilities, no worries. Simply searching for something that helps regulate the nervous system.
2. Identify the dolphins in your life—those who are loyal, playful, fun, inviting, and loving. Turn to these individuals when you're feeling dysregulated, and the contact will be soothing for you.
3. Busy-ness is endorsed in our culture. Be a rebel and pursue stillness in your everyday living.
4. Rest and relaxation is not an option—it's a necessity. To function in our everyday lives, recharging is essential. Schedule down time into your life on a consistent basis and find someone to help you stay accountable for this intention.

5. If you have a loving pet, they are some of the best nervous system regulators. Double up your time with them and notice how you co-regulate each other. If you don't have a pet, borrow one occasionally for your regulation fix.

6. Bookend your day. Create a consistent morning tone setter as well as a bedtime ritual. It doesn't have to be perfect but try to create sacred space for you to listen to the rhythm within.

7. Refer to the Window of Resilience to remind yourself when you are either upregulated or down-regulated. Hold the intention and the efforts to find your way back to the resilience zone more efficiently.

## Reference

Mellody, Pia. 1989. *Breaking Free: A Recovery Workbook for Facing Codependence*. San Francisco: HarperCollins.

# 6 Feeling the Feelings

*I was born with a lot of feelings. As the baby of the family, I lived up to the stereotype of my birth order and was seen as a crybaby at times. Sometimes I knew what I was crying about and at other times I did not. All I knew was that my feelings felt like too much for my parents, and I felt like too much for them to handle.*

*In my childhood home there were either big feelings or no feelings at all. Rage seemed to be the norm, but eventually, I took on the role of mediator, leaving me without access to my wants and desires. None of us were fluent in expressing feelings in a safe and productive way. I learned that it was best to keep my feelings to myself.*

*I thought this would be a wise strategy until my feelings built up pressure, and I learned how to self-soothe through masturbation and eventually through various types of sexual exploration. My guess is that there was a lot of self-soothing going on in my home because we were not equipped to soothe one another.*

*Feelings seemed to go underground and leak out in unexpected ways. Because my parents stayed in a loveless marriage for many years beyond its expiration date, an atmosphere of tension and discontent filled the air. Luckily, a lifetime of therapy and twelve-step programs have helped me thaw from the days when it wasn't safe enough to express myself fully.*

Feelings get a bad rap. Rather than being seen as useful or informative, they are often experienced as a nuisance or something to avoid. People often say, "Don't be sad—pull up your bootstraps." "Don't wear your heart on your sleeve. You're going to get hurt that way." "Tears are a sign of weakness." Many families may be emotionally underdeveloped, which leaves children (or adult children) ill-equipped to navigate the vast world of feelings inside of you.

*I tried hard to put on a happy face. I learned this from my dad. To the outside world he was a dutiful father and husband, but in the home, I saw his sadness, loneliness, and rage. I used to think he was two-faced, but he was simply doing the best he knew under miserable conditions. My dad found solace in his career while raising four challenging sons inside of a crumbling marriage.*

*Feeling my feelings was dangerous territory because I had the idea that if I truly felt the depth of my emotions, I would become unglued. As a young child, I cried a lot to the point where I felt like I couldn't stop. As a teenager, I learned how to hold back the tears, but this also muted other feelings like anger and hurt. We can't turn off our feelings selectively. By bottling up my feelings, I became more frozen and intellectualized, which left me vulnerable to my eventual sexual compulsivity.*

DOI: 10.4324/9781032650487-7

*With the help of several talented therapists, I'm finding safer, more productive ways to share my emotions. Feeling the feelings is not just an idea—it's a road to deeper connection and intimacy especially when you find someone who is curious enough to love you despite your eccentricities.*

Compulsive sexual behavior has been an attempt to regulate your emotions—at times, to feel more and at other times to feel less. In this chapter you'll learn to process them safely and productively. As you get more acquainted with your feelings, you open the door to more authentic relationships both with yourself and others. Here we will focus primarily on anger, hurt, fear and loneliness which can be quite overpowering for many people in recovery.

## Jack's Story: Uncovering Unexpressed Emotions

*Jack grew up in a home where feelings were never expressed through words. His parents had both immigrated from Lithuania to New York and were not fluent with their emotions. Jack was an only child and felt deep shame because he always felt different than his friends. His parents had strong accents and worked long hours in restaurants. Whenever they were home together, they were always bickering.*

*As a teenager, Jack fell into compulsive porn use. The unlimited access to naked images felt comforting and stimulating. His unexpressed feelings were creating more and more internal pressure as he felt profoundly shameful of both his parents and his sexual orientation. Fortunately, he had a compassionate aunt who was a nurse and a confidant. She turned out to be his saving grace who was interested in understanding him and getting to know his suffering. As time progressed, Jack's compulsive porn use was taking up much of his time leaving him lost and lonely, so he decided to seek help through therapy as well as attending a twelve-step meeting designed for gay men. For the first time, Jack started to realize the depth of his feelings and how much they had to teach him.*

If you have ever seen a feelings chart, you know that they illustrate a wide assortment of animated faces representing an array of emotions. In this chapter use this opportunity to identify any thoughts, feelings, or sensations that surface for you. Although there are countless feelings, here are the primary ones:

| Mad | Shame |
|---|---|
| Sad | Guilt |
| Glad | Hurt |
| Afraid | Love/Hate |

We can all benefit from more emotional literacy, and there is no better place to do this than in therapy groups. When orienting someone to join one of my groups, I ask them to consider the following two questions: 1. What are you feeling inside of yourself right now? and 2. How are you feeling toward others at this moment? These are "here and now" questions—a shorthand to ask yourself what is going on inside of you. I encourage you to practice this language because it's a way of creating closeness. If you can take emotional risks and be more vulnerable with others, intimacy and trust will follow. If you are not able to identify a feeling, I encourage you to notice what is happening in your body. Hopefully, the somatic awareness will translate into emotions over time.

Although we aren't going to go into depth in this chapter about codependency, remind yourself that you are never responsible for other people's feelings or reactions. As humans in relationship with other humans, we always influence one another, yet it's not your job to caretake or rescue anyone based on their uncomfortable feelings. If anything, it's a chance for you to be compassionate with them without feeling like you have to save them.

## Accepting Anger as an Ally

*Anger, and most of the time rage, was palpable in my home. My parents were unhappy in their marriage as far back as I can remember, leaving them with a hefty dose of rage and grief. I'm sure there was a time when they had fun and high hopes for a fulfilling life together, but these early dreams were soon replaced with brokenheartedness. I believe my parents did the best they could, and at this point in my life, I don't blame them, although I once did. Retrospectively, I see their challenges and limitations as well as my own, and now is the time for you to investigate how anger works in your life today.*

**Action Step:** How were feelings expressed (or not) in your childhood home?

_____

_____

_____

*As a kid, I avoided anger at all costs. When there was an eruption in the family, and there were many, I went to my room, shut the door and listened to 70s music—possibly Kansas, Yes, or Boston. It was my best attempt to cope at the time but left me utterly alone with my invisible anger and other silent emotions.*

**Action Step:** How did you express or avoid anger as a child?

_____

_____

_____

Unexpressed anger is a slippery slope toward problematic sexual behavior. Retreating to my room and hiding from the brokenheartedness was the best thing I knew how to do back then. Nowadays, I do my best to face my anger directly and find ways to identify and process emotions that were avoided in the past.

**Action Step:** How do you face and process your anger today (or not)?

_____

_____

_____

Here is a well-kept secret. Anger is a life force and a life energy. It's a way of clearly knowing what feels acceptable or unacceptable—okay or not okay—and then setting boundaries based on this awareness. Once you're able to identify your anger, it's possible to express it openly, honestly, and directly. If you're fortunate enough to have someone in your life who is open to listening and understanding you fully, build upon that relationship because safe, productive expressions of anger will bring you even closer together.

**Action Step:** Name at least one person in your life who is able to receive all of your feelings including your anger.

_____

_____

_____

For most of my life I had a very strong need to be liked which I now realize was a way to avoid anger. I used to believe that if I always said "Yes," nobody would be angry with me. Now I know I have options. By responding "Yes," "No" or "Maybe," I ask myself which choice truly fits. Saying "No" ultimately frees up energy and makes room for a bigger "Yes." In other words, I check in with myself to decide how I want to use the time and energy that I gain by saying "No."

Keep in mind that we're not focusing on rage. Rage is typically a destructive or self-destructive form of anger. Often pent-up for an extended period, rage is an extreme dysregulation of the nervous system requiring more attention and deeper healing. If we look underneath rage, you will generally find helplessness, deep hurt, and disillusionment. Anger and rage are cousins, but anger creates bridges while rage burns them down.

Here are some additional action steps to build a stronger relationship with anger:

1. Normalize anger as a natural, necessary emotion. All your feelings are valid and useful. By editing or censoring your anger, you're removing a vital part of yourself.

**Action Step:** Identify and list any current sources of anger.

_____

_____

_____

2. Every family has an anger blueprint—the way anger was expressed in your childhood.

   **Action Step:** Describe how anger was expressed (or not expressed) by you and your family members.

   _____

   _____

   _____

   By identifying when you are angry, you will notice when you fall into old themes and patterns and how to move beyond them.

   **Action Step:** How do you want to express your anger today in safer, productive ways?

   _____

   _____

   _____

   This is not easy to do on your own, and it's an opportunity to ask for help from a therapist or sponsor to guide you along the way.

3. Express your anger by letting others know what feels okay and what doesn't feel okay. This is a hallmark of effective boundaries. By knowing where you end and another person begins, you remain on your side of the street.

   **Action Step:** Identify a current circumstance that feels unacceptable to you right now. Express this to a confidant.

   _____

   _____

   _____

   There will be some trial and error expressing anger so be compassionate with yourself.

4. Distinguish between anger and rage. Anger generally brings people closer, and rage distances you from others. Anger can be direct, clear, and honest whereas rage is messier and often indirect. Pay attention to these emotions and practice authentic conversations with your therapist, sponsor, or loved ones.

5. Keep writing about your anger. By keeping a daily or weekly log, you can process the feelings that are burdensome. If you practice the twelve steps, utilize the fourth and tenth step as a way of staying current with your resentments while processing them as they arise for you.

**Action Step:** What is happening inside of you right now? Identify any anger, crankiness, or irritation you may find. Once you locate it, ask yourself what it may be communicating to you.

_____

_____

_____

6. The full expression of anger is an intimacy-builder. Not everyone has the capacity to process your anger with you but ask those you trust to see if they would be willing to listen to your anger even if it involves them.

**Action Step:** Identify any emotionally reliable people in your life who are capable of listening to your anger.

_____

_____

_____

7. By tracking and expressing anger more freely, you will be less likely to fall into out-of-control sexual behavior. Check in regularly with a confidant, a sponsor, a coach, or a therapist to build connection and open communication. If you do have a slip or recurrence, go back, and see if any unexpressed anger might have been present before the problematic sexual behavior occurred.

### Illuminating Hurt as the Designer Emotion

Surrounded by anger, sadness, disappointment, disillusionment, and shame, hurt is the hub of the wheel.

When you feel deeply hurt, it leaves you with an emotional wound that requires close attention. Using a band-aid won't heal it. You need to irrigate it, change the emotional dressing daily, and give it oxygen until the healing process naturally mends. Sometimes hurt doesn't go away entirely, but instead, it offers perspective and, eventually, less acute pain. What does hurt have to teach you?

*There was an argument on the playground. Charlie fell to the ground after Joey shoved him. "Charlie wouldn't share his potato chips and he hurt my feelings," Joey explained. Charlie cried out, "he made me mad because I was really hungry... and I didn't want to share them."*

This playground conflict illustrates how kids typically blame others and end up pointing the finger elsewhere rather than looking at their own part. As children this is understandable, but many adults still participate in this *shame and blame* game. Nobody can actually make you feel a certain way, so ultimately, it's up to you to take full responsibility for your feelings and reactions. In recovery it requires consistent emotional awareness because unexpressed resentments and hurts can lead to problematic sexual choices. Many adults remain immature and become experts at finger pointing rather than looking within themselves and metabolizing hurt more effectively.

"I'm creating this. It's not the other person's fault." When your feelings are hurt, can you say this to yourself and really mean it? Once you take full responsibility for your feelings, you remove yourself from falling into victim mode. If you're ready to look deeper within yourself, you may realize that these feelings are not something to be worked out with the other person. Instead, it will be more valuable to create a productive inner dialogue.

**Action Step:** Ask yourself if you're feeling hurt right now or in your recent past. Identify the situation or relationship and see if it's possible to take full responsibility for your hurt without blaming the other person.

_____

_____

_____

When the activation from the hurt is still high, perceptions remain distorted—both yours and the other person's. Therefore, this won't be the ideal time to process feelings.

**Action Step:** Acknowledge any current hurt feelings, identify them, and make a list. Be compassionate with yourself as you decide how to proceed.

_____

_____

_____

When your feelings are hurt by someone, you will often try and make meaning out of the other person's behavior. You might find yourself obsessing about the situation, possibly resulting in a feeling of shame or "not being good enough." The other person has no power to do any of this to you so it's up to you to disentangle this emotional knot, often with the wisdom of others.

Another common experience related to hurt feelings results in you generating an illusion of separateness which often manifests in the position of "superior victim." This is a common way of protecting yourself but also creates an artificial separateness from the other person. Getting out of the superior position of self-righteousness allows you to move toward similarities and sameness and possibly resulting in more compassion.

**Action Step:** Identify a time when you were in the superior victim role. It's not always evident at first but be sure to remember a time you were deeply hurt and write about how you fell into this role of both superiority and victimhood.

_____

_____

_____

When you're able to see the sameness between you and others, you will begin to see them as your teacher. You may even start to hold them with positive regard. When your feelings are hurt, the other person becomes a mirror reflecting invisible parts of yourself—a moment to look deeply within.

**Action Step:** Try to locate these hidden parts that the hurtful person reflects upon you. (Hint: These are parts of yourself that you generally don't want to recognize as yours—your so-called *shadow self.*)

_____

_____

_____

Now that you are developing a fresh, new perspective to metabolize hurt, here are some additional action steps to apply to your repertoire of possibilities:

**Action Step:** Identify when you're feeling hurt. Because it's often disguised as sadness, shame, disappointment, disillusionment, or anger, it may go unrecognized. Keep a log of experiences when you feel hurt or when you have possibly hurt someone else. Hurting others is inevitable, and so is being hurt by others. It's not the hurt that counts—it's how you deal with it.

_____

_____

_____

1. Distinguish between resentment and hurt. Generally, resentment is something you feel toward others, and hurt is usually felt from others. Track hurtful and resentful feelings to raise your emotional awareness.

   **Action Step:** What is your relationship with hurt? Identify how you currently relate to it and how you would ideally like to relate to it in the future.

   _____

   _____

   _____

   **Action Step:** What is your relationship with resentment? Identify how you currently relate to it and how you would ideally like to relate to it in the future.

   _____

   _____

   _____

2. Take full responsibility for all your feelings and reactions, paying special attention to hurt feelings. Once you take stock of your feelings and reactions, you will stay out of victim mode and feel more empowered.
3. Try to process the hurt without involving the other person. Most people will be compelled to work things out directly with the party in question. Resist this temptation. It's not their job to work it through with you. Instead, collaborate with a confidant such as your therapist or sponsor as you process hurt.
4. Name your shame that often accompanies hurt. It can be an uphill battle to try and understand the other person's role. As a result, you end up feeling "less than" or "not good enough." Give yourself time to work through the shame as you build more shame resilience.

   **Action Step:** Identify a current or recent hurt feeling and write about the shame associated with it. This will help you distinguish between hurt and shame.

   _____

   _____

   _____

5. Right-size yourself. Hurt often results in you shifting into a superior-victim mode, but condescension and victimhood will only backfire leaving you even

more isolated. Instead, practice self-compassion as well as kindness for the other person which will help you discover greater connection to self, others, and your higher power.

**Action Step:** Repeat to yourself, "May I accept myself fully for exactly who I am at any given moment?" and "May I accept the other person fully for exactly who they are at any given moment?"

_____

_____

_____

6. Practice gratitude for this opportunity to learn about yourself and the value of the other person.

**Action Step:** How has the other person been a teacher for you because of the hurt?

_____

_____

_____

7. Identify ways that you withdraw support from yourself. For instance, you may be obsessing about the hurtful incident and blaming the other person.

**Action Step:** How am I withdrawing support from myself?

_____

_____

_____

8. Reinstate support to yourself with nurturing choices such as Mindful Self-Compassion, radical acceptance, and receiving guidance from others.

**Action Step:** List specific ways you can restore support to yourself at this time.

_____

_____

_____

Many of us have been taught from a very young age to say we're sorry and work things out with the person who hurt you. This is not my philosophy. The strategies mentioned earlier in this chapter offer an alternative way to heal hurt from the inside out. Of course, it may be helpful at some point to talk to the other person once you have the chance to work things out within yourself, but don't bypass the opportunity to work on this internally. Invite trusted loved ones to your grown-up playground and see how radical compassion works for you over time.

### Facing Tiers of Fears

Although fear and anxiety are close cousins, fear lets you know that there is some type of actual or perceived danger while anxiety tends to be the body's natural reaction to stress. For this chapter, I will simply refer to fear as the feeling and anxiety as a mind-body reaction.

**Action Step**: How was fear expressed (or not) in your childhood home?

_____

_____

_____

**Action Step:** How do you express fear (or not) currently?

_____

_____

_____

**Action Step:** How would you ideally like to respond to fear in the future?

_____

_____

_____

There is a myth that fear is a negative emotion. I don't categorize feelings as positive or negative because they all have value. Anger, hurt, and fear may be challenging for you in different ways, but they all provide opportunities to learn about yourself and build emotional resilience. Here are a few strategies for fear and anxiety relief—how many do you use?

- Individual and group psychotherapy.
- Physical exercise/movement.
- Nutritional balance.
- Consistent sleep habits.

- Yoga.
- Meditation.
- Breathwork.
- Somatic awareness: Somatic Experiencing and Brainspotting.
- Books and articles related to fear and anxiety relief.
- Practice imperfection.
- Practice gratitude.
- Explore spirituality (whatever gives your life meaning).
- Cultivate humor, play, and laughter.
- Spend quality time with pets.
- Carve out downtime daily/schedule time off.
- Unplug from technology.
- Volunteer/be of service.
- Music: listen, play, sing.
- Develop nurturing self-talk. (For example: I'll do the best I can for today.)
- Therapeutic massage/somatic bodywork.
- Progressive relaxation/visualization/guided imagery.
- Build self-awareness and track anxiety triggers.
- Practice self-acceptance and self-compassion.
- Homeopathic/Ayurvedic/naturopathic medicine/psychopharmacology.

Meditation is a time-tested, evidence-based strategy for anxiety relief which has been with us for thousands of years. If you are already meditating, challenge yourself to expand your practice. If you're not meditating currently, why not? Not only is it more and more available in our communities, but there are many on-line opportunities as well. Meditation is one of the most beneficial anti-anxiety *medications* on the market available without a prescription. When your anxiety is down, your emotional resilience will strengthen and so will your overall well-being.

## Combating Loneliness and Isolation

Before we wind down our exploration of emotions, I'd like to share a reminder related to the original subtitle of my book: *Moving from Isolation to Intimacy.* It's not helpful to be a lone ranger. On the one hand, loneliness is part of life. Whether you're surrounded by others on a consistent basis, or you are working alone from home, loneliness, sadness, and isolation are inevitable. How you choose to connect with others and create deeper contact is vital. It's not about the quantity of people in your life as much as it's about creating high-quality, meaningful connections. As Johann Hari reminds us, "The opposite of addiction isn't sobriety. The opposite of addiction is connection." Evidently, the same can be said about loneliness and sadness. The opposite of loneliness and isolation is connection.

What if you could be good company for yourself? Would it be possible to enjoy your solitude? Loneliness is part of life, but it's also possible to learn to savor your time with yourself. When I turned forty, I spent some time with my coach in the lake region of Northern Italy and the remaining time of my Italian adventure by myself. It wasn't easy for me to travel alone but as the trip unfolded, I found my true vacation rhythm and actually found the experience liberating. At age forty I was beginning to feel like a capable, competent person.

**Action Step**: Describe a recent experience of loneliness.

_____

_____

_____

**Action Step:** As you reflect on that moment, what would be a kind way to talk with yourself about your loneliness?

_____

_____

_____

In the twelve-step rooms, there is a common reminder that "This too shall pass," and this applies to feelings as well. If you're feeling stuck in your emotions for too long, that's generally a sign to seek professional help. Murakami reminds us that "Pain is inevitable, suffering is optional." Therefore, emotional pain is part of healing, but if you find yourself suffering for extended periods of time, it's an indication that asking for more help is vital.

## Your Practice

1. Feelings are like clouds. They may seem like they are stalling at times but eventually they move through and disperse. Remind yourself that an individual feeling is not here to stay—it's just here to teach you about yourself.
2. Unexpressed feelings tend to be dangerous if not processed. Unprocessed feelings may lead to sexualizing your feelings. Do whatever it takes to process them more efficiently.
3. Anger gets a bad rap. It's an indication that something feels unacceptable or "not okay" with you. When you identify anger and ground yourself, this is the time to set a boundary that works better for you.
4. Conflict avoidance generally comes from fear. Identify your fear and try to understand the conflict that exists within you.

5. Anger creates connection. Find the people in your life who are truly available to listen and validate your anger. Anger can be a bid for contact.

6. Hurt is a multi-dimensional feeling which may involve anger, sadness, fear, resentment, and disillusionment. Embrace hurt as one of your greatest teachers and work toward keeping your side of the street clean.

## References

Hari, Johann. 2016. *Chasing the Scream: The First and Last Days of the War on Drugs*. London: Bloomsbury.

Murakami, Haruki. 2008. *What I Talk About When I Talk About Running*. New York: Knopf.

# 7 Cultivating Contentment

There is nothing wrong with suffering—it's a natural part of being human. Some cultures define themselves through tragedy, beginning with Greece and neighboring countries in both Western and Eastern Europe. On the other hand, the United States has been cultivating a *happiness culture* focusing on joy-seeking and distress reduction which sometimes leads to escape behaviors. Happiness is a wonderful aspiration, but it cannot be the whole story.

*In 2000 I met my coach, Sam, who was on the faculty of my coach training program. I was introduced to the brand-new field of Positive Psychology: "The Science of Happiness." Although Sam and I primarily focused on my core values and future goals, she wasn't afraid to help me look at the barriers to my happiness—typically stale messages and old fears from my past. I found it was impossible to experience gratitude, purpose, and direction without keeping an eye on my trauma reactions. Even the father of Positive Psychology, Dr. Martin Seligman, started his career studying learned helplessness, which he eventually turned upside down to study learned optimism. Therefore, contentment and suffering can coexist—it doesn't have to be one or the other, but where we choose to focus our attention grows exponentially.*

*Today I hold my childhood trauma with a lighter touch. Acceptance, connection, and love get more of my attention. When I fall into a trauma reaction, I try to be curious and nonjudgmental, being the best parent to the little kid inside me. When I'm spending a nourishing afternoon with a friend or playing with my dog, I do my best to savor those experiences and not take them for granted. In other words, savoring contentment is a daily practice which also helps me keep an eye on the brokenheartedness in the rearview mirror.*

## Identifying Core Values

Effective coaching is a future-focused, action-oriented process that begins with values clarification. Purposeful goals along with a clear-cut vision can only take shape after you've grounded yourself in core values.

**Action Step:** Ask yourself the following question repeatedly until you run out of answers: "What matters most to me?" (a version of values clarification). For example, my priorities are relationships, love, and ease. It took me several years to understand these core values, and now I realize that all my actions need to be congruent with these items for me to feel deeper contentment. If you're not

DOI: 10.4324/9781032650487-8

congruent with your core values, it will be difficult to clarify goals and create an authentic vision.

**Action Step:** Here is another Values Clarification exercise. In this chapter of your life, what values resonate the most to you? Choose five to ten core values.

| | |
|---|---|
| Humor | Fun |
| Directness | Participation |
| Contentment | Collaboration |
| Productivity | Community |
| Love | Connectedness |
| Service | Ease |
| Contribution | Spirituality |
| Excellence | Empowerment |
| Free spirit | Full self-expression |
| Focus | Integrity |
| Harmony | Creativity |
| Accomplishment | Independence |
| Leadership | Nurturing |
| Honesty | Joy |
| Adventure | Authenticity |
| Lack of pretense | Risk-taking |
| Tradition | Peace |
| Growth | Vitality |

Because there tends to be some confusion between coaching and therapy, I thought I would take a moment to describe these two overlapping yet contrasting modalities. Today most people know when to seek therapy but coaching still remains misunderstood at times.

Coaching began in the corporate sector back in the 1970s and 1980s when it became clear that executives and corporate leaders could benefit from consultants helping them refine their "people" skills. And then life coaching took off in the 1990s as elements of executive coaching were adapted to working one-on-one with a focus on life goals. In the past few years coaching has taken shape as a new voice in the addiction recovery community as it's now available to individuals in any stage of recovery as well as in many residential treatment centers around the country and internationally.

If a client seeks coaching but instead focuses exclusively on a recent crisis or emotional pain, they're probably more appropriate for therapy. On the other hand, a coaching client needs to be able to identify specific goals for their future and to be open and willing to collaborate with a coach. As you can see, coaching and therapy can work quite well side by side. Coaches focus on leveraging strengths with the attention always given to your unique talents. These qualities may also be recognized in psychotherapy, but this is a primary emphasis for coaches. Coaches also help you identify values, priorities, and goals and hold these intentions to help you stay on track. In other words, coaching is an opportunity to design a fresh roadmap for this next chapter of recovery and then guides you to stay accountable toward your bigger vision.

**Action Step:** Who would you like to invite into your corner at this time? A coach? A therapist? A sponsor? A pastor? A close friend? I have found that I've needed different support at different times of my recovery. Take a moment and ask yourself who you would like to invite on to your recovery team at this time.

_____

_____

_____

*Dating back to my turbulent childhood, I've always struggled with the idea of happiness although I do have many fond memories thanks to loving friends. On the inside of my home, I witnessed chronic suffering. My childhood wasn't a happy time, but somehow, I managed to shut the door to my bedroom and create a mini-sanctuary equipped with my black-and-white TV and Siberian husky, Nikki—all survival strategies.*

*Throughout my childhood I was adopted by several families who must have detected the misery in my home. From an early age my surrogate families demonstrated several versions of happiness that showed me the possibilities of joy.*

*Fast-forward to my life as an adult, and sustained happiness remains elusive. I've learned to find moments of joy with friends and family of choice, and I'm grateful that my sense of humor and laughter are intact although I continue to take myself way too seriously. Yet, like most of us, I remain a work in progress.*

When I met my coach the direction of my career shifted in profound ways. She believed in me more than I believed in myself at the time. Sam also reminded me that "It's not that anything has to happen but simply what could happen." For a recovering perfectionist, those were soothing words. It was the first time I was encouraged to open the aperture to the limitless possibilities in front of me. All the while contentment and life satisfaction were in the forefront of this brand-new expedition.

Through the years Sam has helped me refine my core values, explore my purpose, and examine where and how I choose to invest my energy. Most recently, we focused on my book, *It's Not About the Sex* and how I wanted to spread the word of this grassroots project. After an intensive weekend of soul-searching, I realized that these words captured the process: *love, ease, fun, and play.* These simple words have become touchstones both for the book project as well as my life and career in general.

In contrast to my esteemed happiness researchers, I've adopted the word *contentment* which seems to relieve the pressure sometimes associated with happiness or joy. Don't get me wrong, I do have moments of joy, and I'm very grateful for those moments, but contentment seems more realistic and sustainable for me.

Being comfortable in my own skin. Allowing myself to read a book, walk the dog, watch a movie. I aspire to cultivate more contentment.

## Lydia's Story: Understanding Happiness vs. Contentment

*Lydia grew up in Washington Heights in upper Manhattan in the 70s and nothing came easily to her family. She was born in New York after her parents immigrated from the Dominican Republic, and she only has a memory of getting by hand to mouth. There were pleasant memories of playing with neighborhood kids and big family gatherings but there was always a lot of financial stress and worry where the next meal would be coming from.*

*When Lydia became a teenager, she started getting attention from boys and girls alike and realized she could earn money for sexual favors. When she turned twenty-five, she met a man a few years older who she wanted to date. This was a new experience for her, and Lydia realized she wanted to give up the sex work and move forward with her life.*

*After joining SLAA (Sex and Love Addicts Anonymous), she learned that her sexual choices had become compulsive and now she was looking for real intimacy and contentment. When I asked her about the possibility of finding happiness, she shrugged and told me that was a foreign concept. Instead, we landed on the word "contentment" which was much more palatable to her. This is where her work in therapy began.*

**Action step:** When you take a moment to focus on contentment, what images, memories, or ideas come to mind?

_____

_____

_____

**Action Step:** What is one small step toward contentment that you can take that would make the biggest difference?

_____

_____

_____

**Action Step:** Sexual satisfaction is a vital component of life satisfaction. What are your core sexual values? (Playful, fun, safe.)

_____

_____

_____

**Action Step:** When you name your core sexual values, what happens internally? (For example: turned on, hopeful, shut down, scared?)

_____

_____

_____

## Constructing Purposeful Goals

Goals are based on values. Once you clarify your overall values or your sexual values, you are on your way to creating a direction that works for you. As Sam instilled in me, "It's not that anything has to happen, but simply what could happen." Allow yourself to develop stretch goals which may or may not be reachable at this time and develop realistic goals to build your confidence.

**Action Step**: In your heart of hearts, what do you really desire? This is a big goal-oriented question that deserves plenty of time and space to explore. Consider what you want physically, emotionally, mentally, spiritually, and sexually?

_____

_____

_____

**Action Step:** Martin Seligman, the father of Positive Psychology, believes that meaning and engagement are two of the pillars for sustainable happiness. What gives your life meaning? What activities and relationships are engaging and enriching for you?

_____

_____

_____

**Action Step:** On the flip side, if something is not meaningful or engaging, why do you continue to do it? Are you willing to limit or end these activities or relationships?

_____

_____

_____

## Creating Your Recovery Vision

**Action Step:** Take plenty of time and space for this exercise. Go to an inspiring spot to begin to meditate and write. The first time I did this exercise I took two weeks to complete it and took it with me on a few local hikes. It's a dynamic process that will evolve over time, but you can start by asking the following questions:

What do you really, really want and desire? Write about these seven areas. Even if it's not fully possible now, allow yourself to play with the possibilities:

- Health: physical, mental, spiritual sexual.
- Relationships.
- Personal growth.
- Volunteering and being of service.
- Money and finances.
- Work.
- Free time/time off.

Once you've completed this exercise, share it with a trusted confidant.

**Action Step:** We are biologically wired for connection. Therefore, your nervous system and your brain circuitry lights up when you find truly reliable people. Who do you trust the most in your life today? Who can you be yourself with? Build more contact with them. If you're having difficulty identifying a dependable individual, begin with a sponsor, coach, or therapist. Contentment grows when you surround yourself with those you can count on.

_____

_____

**Action Step:** Your relationship with yourself is key to creating your recovery vision. Self-compassion leads to deeper contentment along with self-awareness and self-acceptance. Listen to Mindful Self-Compassion teachers. What steps are you willing to take to bring more self-compassion into your life?

_____

_____

**Action Step:** If you don't have a pet, consider adopting. If you do have a pet, spend more quality time with them and savor the 24/7 entertainment, unconditional love and play they gladly bring to you. How might you create more contact with your pet or other animals?

_____

_____

**Action Step:** Contentment thrives on fun, play, laughter, and humor. Spend time with lighthearted people. Watch comedies or funny videos. Adopt a pet and let your inner child play. Track how much or how little you are laughing each day. What are you willing to do to enhance fun and play in your recovery?

_____

_____

_____

## Giving Gratitude

Appreciating the little things in life is where gratitude begins. Aaron Copeland's famous piece *Simple Gifts* refers to love and delight that surrounds us if we take the time to notice it. It's a mindfulness exercise that is available to us anytime we open our eyes to it.

*A few years ago, I travelled to Boise to attend my little cousin's college graduation. In all honesty, my little cousin is now 6'5," but he will always be my "little cousin" because I met him the day he was born, and he was quite little at the time! Although he now towers over me, he's a gentle giant with a heart of gold, and celebrating his entry into the world brought me immense pride and gratitude.*

*Unfortunately, the current state of our world is complex, and it's not always easy for me to access the gratitude within. But it's all around us if we keep our eyes and hearts open to it. If I pay attention and focus on gratitude, it will always appear and expand. And it's truly a practice.*

*So, there I am in the arena at Boise State watching my little cousin graduate with honors among more than 2000 other graduates. He has chosen education as his career path, and I couldn't be prouder of him. To be a part of his early life when he lived in Los Angeles and now to see him grow up in Idaho brings me waves of gratitude. Grateful to move through life with him even if he is a two-hour flight away. Grateful to see him find his way through some challenging times and to see him thrive both academically and as a human being. Grateful to see him discover his passion both as a teacher and as a lover of life. My little cousin is not only a high school teacher but also my teacher. Teaching me to appreciate the long-distance family relationship and love that endures.*

## Your Practice

1. Contentment is only one dimension of the human condition. Holding the intention for happiness, joy or contentment allows you to keep your eye on this part of you.
2. Core values and sexual values help you soul-search what really matters most to you. Not to our culture, not to our families, not to anybody else, but to you.

3. Goals and intentions give you room to play with the infinite possibilities in front of you. The good news is that you're never locked into anything. They simply offer a direction which can be re-navigated at any time.
4. Visioning is an opportunity to open the aperture and see what you might want to explore.
5. Gratitude provides the glue to contentment and inner peace.

# 8 Restoring Purpose

*I believe I was put on this planet to help others. Not only helping others heal their past but also finding a future that matters to them. I realized this as a young child as I unconsciously assumed the role of arbitrator in my family as well as the counselor to neighborhood moms, teachers, and even crossing guards. When someone asks me when I knew I wanted to be a therapist, I jokingly say "in utero," but there is truth to it. Born into my chaotic family and falling into the role of a parentified kid, it was truly my destiny, and it took time to integrate my native talents into a meaningful career.*

*The exploration of purpose was introduced to me by my coach, Sam, in 2001, as I grappled with career direction at the time. In its simplest form, purpose is based on your core values which are based on what matters most to you. Nowadays I understand that my superpower is helping others to feel heard, understood and seen, and my grandmother planted the original seeds. Whenever I spent time with my grandma, I felt deeply loved and lovable, and I try to pay it forward and spread the love wherever I go.*

*Building better boundaries has always been one of my biggest challenges as I need to pay attention to my emotional limits. Saying "No" still isn't easy, but I try to be clear with myself and others by saying no when I need to say no. Yet, I still feel guilty at times which is a lasting echo of my past. I wish I could say that every day I stick to my purpose, but instead, it's an intention I hold firmly.*

Let's talk about cultivating purpose after your problematic sexual behavior has diminished. Although there can be the excitement of a blank canvas, it can also be quite overwhelming and uncertain. Now that the compulsive sex has ended, who am I? What do I really want and desire? What matters most to me? If you're open to considering these existential questions, they open a spiritual dialogue of exploration. Out-of-control sexual behavior was often about the absence of purpose, and sustainable recovery requires your quest for meaning.

Viktor Frankl, a psychiatrist and Holocaust survivor, developed a branch of psychology called Logotherapy. His book, *Man's Search for Meaning* holds the premise that our primary motivational force is to discover meaning in life. Whether it be a global tragedy such as the Holocaust or a more private anguish, he believes it's your birthright to grapple with the meaning of your life.

DOI: 10.4324/9781032650487-9

My grandmother was raised on a farm in Romania in the early twentieth century. After immigrating to Brooklyn, she eventually migrated to my hometown in South Jersey where she lived a humble life including simple gifts such as playing gin rummy, preparing my favorite salmon croquettes, and taking family trips to Atlantic City. These may seem like mundane moments, but the love she effusively shared with me set the stage for my focus on deeper connection and generosity.

Many years ago, I went to a workshop at UCLA on spirituality and addiction, and the chaplain told the audience that spirituality can be defined as *whatever gives your life meaning.* When I heard him speak, I reflected on my relationship with my grandmother and eventually, with the help of my coach, I developed a mission statement as follows:

To encourage, affirm, and inspire meaningful connection, ongoing learning, and deeper growth both in myself and others. To invite love, ease and play into all my relationships.

In my book, *It's Not About the Sex: Moving from Isolation to Intimacy after Sexual Addiction,* here are some of the meaningful themes expressed by those I interviewed: Connecting to others, connecting through prayer and meditation, volunteering, being of service, helping others, being kind, participating rather than observing, giving gratitude. Discovering one's purpose is not an overnight venture, it requires ongoing soul-searching, asking the bigger question: "What makes your life worth living?"

## José's Story: Imagining Purpose

*José was raised by hard-working, immigrant parents who moved to Los Angeles from their small town in Mexico. They fought to bring their family to America and made many sacrifices along the way, including leaving some loved ones behind. José received the message that hard work and sacrifice are core values, and he cannot ask for anything greater than the freedom to live here.*

*Shortly into his therapy, he revealed that his father was a functioning alcoholic, and José learned not to say anything for fear he would be punished. As in many alcoholic families, there are challenges with expressing oneself, trusting others, identifying feelings, and questioning the alcoholic's behavior. José became hooked on porn as a teenager which was soothing, secretive, and shameful.*

*Through the help of a friend, José attended SAA (Sex Addicts Anonymous) and eventually ended his relationship with porn. Now that porn was out of the way, we started to have honest conversations about meaning and purpose. José confided that he always wanted to be a paramedic because he knew he was skillful in crisis situations and wanted to help others at times of crisis. His purpose began to take shape accordingly.*

Here are some soul-searching strategies to examine what purpose really means to you.

**Action Step:** What matters most to you? Without overthinking it, write down whatever comes to your mind. This exercise will clarify your values as you examine what gives your life purpose. Hint: Consider the simple gifts.

_____

_____

_____

**Action Step:** Think about a person you love and what seems to give their life meaning. This person may be alive or deceased, but either way they need to be someone you trust and respect. Make a list of things that appear meaningful to them. These items will give you a solid example of what gives others a reason to wake up in the morning.

_____

_____

_____

**Action Step:** How do you give back to others or not? Smiling at your neighbors or volunteering at your local animal shelter are both legitimate examples. Track any acts of kindness and additional ways you would like to be of service. By giving back, you will automatically find meaning within yourself.

_____

_____

_____

**Action Step:** What are you grateful for in your life? For the next twenty-one days (or one week if that feels like too much), make a gratitude list each morning. Those items will reveal possibilities of what gives your life meaning.

_____

_____

_____

**Action Step:** Who do you feel most connected to? Who tends to be most emotionally dependable? Friends, family, co-workers, pets? Ponder this question to determine where the deeper contact in your life exists. These are the people or animals who provide greater meaning.

_____

_____

_____

**Action Step:** A mission statement provides direction and purpose. If your actions and core values are congruent, you'll move forward more easily. If you feel inclined to write a mission statement, you might consider the following formula: Actions + Values + Receivers = Your mission.

_____

_____

_____

**Awareness Step:** Finding purpose in recovery is an unfolding process. Be patient and stay open-hearted to the limitless possibilities.

## Contemplating Spirituality

**Action Step:** Do you resonate with the term "a power greater than yourself"? After many years of going back and forth, I use the word God to describe this, and this may show up through loved ones, my dog, or the Pacific Ocean. How would you describe a power greater than yourself?

_____

_____

_____

Religion and spirituality are often confused. In its simplest description, religion is usually an organized system of faith and worship. Depending on religious tradition, there may be a place of worship where congregants get together. At times, there can be a dogmatic approach which may result in religious trauma and deeply painful suffering. If you believe you suffer from religious trauma, find a therapist who specializes in CSBD and trauma so you can receive the specialized healing you deserve. On the other hand, spirituality focuses on inner peace and purpose and often requires an individual practice.

**Action Step:** Do you believe in spirituality? If so, how would you describe spirituality in your life? Keep in mind that it can be as simple as "whatever gives your life meaning."

_____

_____

_____

**Action Step:** As a child, were you raised with religion or any spiritual practices? If so, what was your upbringing?

_____

_____

_____

**Action step:** If you were raised with a religious framework, what were the takeaways?

_____

_____

_____

**Action Step:** Was it dogmatic or abusive in any way? If so, how?

_____

_____

_____

How does spirituality fit into your recovery today?

_____

_____

_____

*We are not human beings having a spiritual experience. We are spiritual beings having a human experience.*—Pierre Teilhard de Chardin

**Action Step:** How does that quote resonate for you or not?

_____

_____

_____

## Finding a Reason to Wake up in the Morning

Compulsive sexual behavior distracts and avoids. It may distract you from painful or unexpressed feelings, and inevitably it takes you away from being in the here and now. Usually, it's a sign of something I haven't fully expressed so I know it's essential to share what isn't being shared.

Through the years I've learned that my reason to wake up in the morning boils down to meaningful relationships, whether they be with friends, family, or clients. I'm lucky that I have a career that challenges me to establish intimate relationships all the time. And ultimately, I see therapy as a place to learn about love and being the best person you know how to be, whatever that means to you.

Traditionally, twelve-step programs describe addiction with borrowed language from the medical model such as disease, illness, and even the word addiction itself. Yet, there's less shameful and stigmatizing ways to talk about it.

In 1998, Dr. Marty Seligman, a psychologist at the University of Pennsylvania coined the term Positive Psychology, and a like-minded, international community of researchers came out of the woodwork. Not only did they open the door to expanded research in this brand-new field, but they also paved the way toward its application toward addictive, compulsive behaviors.

Instead of focusing on what's wrong with clients, Positive Psychologists began to talk about what's right. Exploring strengths became center stage, and existential-spiritual questions such as "What gives you a reason to wake up in the morning"? and "What makes life worth living?" became part of the new dialogue.

Positive Psychology is a future-focused, action-oriented, wellness model focusing on purpose, resilience, and resourcefulness. Rather than solely focusing on deficits, signature strengths get fully explored, and these are all essential ingredients for sustainable recovery.

Now that you have chosen to stop your out-of-control behaviors, there is room to experience a bigger life with greater possibilities. In early recovery, you acknowledged your tendencies to self-attack and self-sabotage, and eventually, it was time to leverage your resources and identify your deeper wants and desires. Milestones of long-term recovery include emotional resilience, meaningful connection, gratitude, joy, and contentment—all elements related to Positive Psychology.

In the twelve-step rooms, newcomers often focus more on the problem rather than the solution. Taking the lead from old-timers as well as Positive Psychology, it would be remarkable to see what would happen if meetings would focus more on purpose, priorities, and possibilities.

In addition to traditional resentment inventories, develop a joy and gratitude inventory to complement your fourth step. Begin with an early memory of joy or gratitude, and list as many memories as possible. Focus on positive life events to carve out new neural pathways as well as greater awareness of pleasant life events.

Deepak Chopra's book *Overcoming Addictions* states that the absence of joy is the cause and the effect of addiction. This reminds us that joy can be a safety net from future problematic behaviors. As joy becomes a practice, here is a litmus test for you. Does this person, place, thing, or experience nourish or deplete you? Ask yourself this question on a regular basis to reveal what belongs in your life or not.

Twelve-step wisdom reminds you that there are Three *S*'s—service, spirituality, and self-care—all fundamental elements leading to greater contentment. Being of **service** is an antidote to self-centeredness. Spirituality provides meaning and self-care makes it possible to have vitality in all other aspects of life.

**Action Step:** What is your reason to wake up in the morning? If you can't identify a reason, has there ever been a reason?

_____

_____

_____

Because this is a provocative and contemplative question, you may consider working with a coach who can be in your corner as you explore these bigger questions.

**Action Step:** What do you envision as meaningful and purposeful in the future?

Meaning, purpose, and legacy are all big concepts that respond to stillness, soul-searching and playing with the possibilities. It's okay if you don't have clarity in these areas—sometimes I am still working on them. Start with curiosity and try to be nonjudgmental as you consider how these existential beliefs take shape.

## Discovering Legacy

**Action Step:** If you imagine a purposeful life, what might that include?

_____

_____

_____

Legacy generally refers to what you leave behind after death, but for a moment let's consider the type of legacy you may live each day. You may think about it either way, but let's start with today.

**Action Step:** Have you ever thought about your legacy? If so, what is the legacy that you may be cultivating in your life today?

_____

_____

_____

**Action Step:** If you look back on your life from your final days, how would you like to be remembered? In other words, what will you see as your legacy you're leaving behind?

The topics in this chapter can feel lighter or heavier depending on your familiarity with these items. Consult with an emotionally reliable person to explore these big-ticket items.

## Your Practice

1. Ask yourself what gives your life meaning. This will reveal your current version of spirituality. Allow your investigation to change over time.
2. Being of service is a foundational way of creating purpose in your life. Take a look at how you are being other-centered and enjoy the generosity within yourself.
3. Consider all of the possible ways to create meaning in your life. You will find a reason to wake up in the morning when it's not all about you.
4. Consider collaborating with a coach or a trusted confidant as you move toward your bigger intentions.
5. Knowing that these concepts can be amorphous, stay open-minded to the endless possibilities in front of you.

## References

Chopra, Deepak. 1998. *Overcoming Addictions: The Spiritual Solution*. New York: Harmony Books.
Frankl, Viktor. 1949. *Man's Search for Meaning*. Boston: Beacon Press.

# 9 Receiving Love

## Demystifying Attachment Styles

*Obsession has always been one of my favorite escape routes from feeling my feelings. Obsession and fantasy involve imagining things that are improbable, and I became hooked on the thrill-seeking that goes along with the hunt for an unlikely conquest. This quest may be sexual, or it may be romantic, but it almost always stems from attachment ruptures. In fourth grade Melissa was a girl who reminded me of Snow White and the perfection of both etiquette and appearance. I was drawn to her beauty, grace, and ease—obsessed with the idea of Melissa, not the real person because I didn't know her very well. Yet, I idealized her and saw her as an escape from all my problems—the first in a string of romantic obsessions that was going to make my pain go away.*

*Ironically, I had no clue how to approach Melissa, so I stumbled and fumbled until she would go to the movies with me. I wish I could say that this fantasy/obsession cycle went away, but it followed me into adulthood. When I get lost in fantasy, it's an attempt to feel better like any drug, but it's also a reminder to look at what's missing or painful inside of me. Generally, if I'm feeling more nourished in my life, there will be less obsession. If I'm feeling depleted, obsession grows.*

*The moral of the story is that compulsive sexual tendencies often involve obsession but it's not about the obsession or the fantasy. It's an attempt to escape reality and jump into an alternate universe which provides a temporary salve to the pain.*

*Because my nervous system seemed to thaw around age forty as a by-product of my somatic trainings, I now realize I had been living with a highly dysregulated nervous system at the height of my compulsive sexual behavior. It may have looked like I was having lots of fun and enjoying plenty of sex, but there was very little pleasure associated with it.*

*In my elementary school days sex education was anatomical at best and I don't remember either of my parents talking with me about sex or my body. Like my siblings and many of my friends, we were on our own to discover the mysteries of sex and sexuality without guidance. It was a crapshoot from the beginning.*

*On the other hand, compulsive sexual exploration provided me with information about my turn-ons, turn-offs, and desires. Keep in mind that most of this happened during the 80s and early 90s when AIDS had just emerged as a pandemic. As a result, I was nervous, scared, and overwhelmed—never a helpful combination for relaxed, hot, sexual experiences.*

DOI: 10.4324/9781032650487-10

*Nowadays I've been revisiting my sexual desires as well as the erotic conflicts that have been in the way of examining what pleasure really means to me. Even after all this time, I still feel like a teenager when it comes to understanding my erotic template and my sexual roadmap. Discovering what I missed out on and considering what I would like to explore leaves me with both regret and hope in this chapter of my life.*

**Action Step:** How do you relate to this story? What associations do you have?

_____

_____

_____

## Confronting Intimacy Avoidance

Scratch the surface of compulsive sexual behavior, and you'll find an avoidant attachment style underneath. As a matter of fact, sexual compulsivity and intimacy avoidance are inseparable. Because you had poor role models to show you the way, substantial intimacy blocks are inevitable. Keep in mind that these barriers have also served as survival strategies. Historically, giving and receiving love has been dangerous territory resulting in brokenheartedness and profound isolation.

**Action Step:** Do you consider yourself to have intimacy challenges? How do you describe your style of avoidance? Hint: Intimacy avoidance is universal.

_____

_____

_____

How you experienced love and attunement in the first months and years of life lays the blueprint for your style of relating to others as a grown-up. Early attachment experiences lay the groundwork for your grown-up attachment patterns. One of the keys to sustainable recovery is to integrate sex, love, and intimacy. In the movie *Moulin Rouge*, the protagonist, Christian, declares that "the greatest thing you'll ever learn is just to love and be loved in return." Because of my own challenges with intimacy—both longing for and fearing closeness—this was a very moving message in the film as he desperately pursued love with someone who was truly unavailable and potentially life-threatening to him.

Christian's anguish escalated when ongoing attempts to establish deeper contact with his object of desire remained futile. The obsessive quest for the unavailable person—sometimes referred to as *impossible love*—creates emotional hunger and unsatisfied longings. Giving and receiving love more freely is a powerful antidote to compulsive behavior because it calms the nervous system and creates new neural pathways of feeling lovable. When you're able to develop true intimate contact with others, seeking impossible love loses steam, and sobriety gains traction.

**Action Step:** How do you relate to Christian or not? His character was starving for love which illustrates a part of all of us.

_____

_____

_____

Jan Bauer's book, *Impossible Love*, describes both the suffering and the growing edge that goes along with looking for love in all the wrong places—for example, affairs and emotional entanglements. Although the excitement of the brief adrenaline rush may be supercharged, it's unlikely to be converted into long-term intimacy. Don't get me wrong. The impossible love can be a fantastic learning opportunity, but only if you're able to recognize it, gain perspective on your part in the relationship and tease out the deeper meaning and purpose beneath your longings.

**Action Step:** Most of us can identify an "impossible love" in our lifetime. Who was your impossible love and what did you learn about yourself because of this experience?

_____

_____

_____

If you have the luxury of owning a pet, this is one of the finest intimacy laboratories. My dogs have always been instrumental in my practice of giving and receiving. Pets are powerful healers because of their instinctual way of loving. And if you pay attention to the free flow of love they offer, they demonstrate a rare template of intimacy unsurpassed by humans. No expectations. No conditions. No pressure. Pets offer a rare 24/7 consistency as a true companion and whole-hearted creature.

**Action Step:** If you have a pet, describe this love relationship. How do you give love to your canine friend? How do you withhold love? How do you receive love?

_____

_____

_____

Because we are *most defended against our greatest needs,* intimacy can be an emotionally precarious territory. Over time, you learned to build self-protective walls due to past hurts, disappointments, and intrusions, but in recovery the challenge and the opportunity is to safely break down your walls and learn to rely on others gradually. If you're determined to heal old relationship wounds, being in a relationship is the best place to work on them—whether it be romantic, friendship, or family. As you step into the healing properties of emotionally reliable relationships, avoidance will fade away making room for trust and respect to grow. Walking through your fears and vulnerabilities will promote deeper contact and healthier versions of relationships.

**Action Step:** Describe your current emotional walls. In other words, how are you keeping loved ones at a distance?

_____

_____

_____

**Action Step:** Who are the most emotionally dependable people in your life today? They may be a teacher, friend, coach, sponsor, or therapist.

_____

_____

_____

All of us come into the world defenseless and vulnerable, and in the best of circumstances, we have a *good enough parent*, as psychoanalyst Donald Winnicott described. Many of us had the necessities of shelter and food, but true emotional nourishment was often lacking or intermittent at best. This leaves the child with self-blame and complicated questions such as: *Am I doing something wrong? Am I lovable?* Of course, these questions are unconscious stories that the malnourished child is making up about the lack of consistent, unconditional love available to him. Eventually, the child simply gives up.

## Justin's Story: Unearthing Avoidant Attachment

*"I don't understand intimacy. No matter what I do, I always feel suffocated with the women I date. They always seem to be unavailable, and I have no idea what I'm doing wrong."*

*During Justin's childhood, his parents were unhappy and distant from one another. Instead of looking to her husband for emotional support, his mother inappropriately leaned on Justin as a confidant. Though he found her smothering at times, Justin felt important and liked the attention. As a teenager, he became more uneasy with this surrogate husband role but still felt loyal to her. Justin's father colluded with this arrangement because he felt less pressure to show up fully in the marriage. Through the years he had multiple affairs.*

*Relationships always felt complicated and burdensome to Justin. In his twenties, he only dated older, married women. Unconsciously, he chose unstable relationships that always ended painfully. Justin's dating pattern kept him at a safe distance from real intimacy. In some ways, this felt comfortable and familiar. Yet, in other ways it left him profoundly lonely.*

*After several failed relationships, he finally went to therapy and began to identify and understand his avoidant-attachment style. Justin began to date single women, but when he felt close to a girlfriend, he would always feel suffocated by them. He would then sabotage it through excessive use of porn and escorts—anything to create distance. As the out-of-control sexual behaviors became more frequent, he grew more frustrated.*

*Justin was longing for deeper connection, but his intimacy-avoidance left him hungry. At thirty-two, Justin attended his first SLAA meeting, and his quest for deeper healing began.*

Regulating emotional distance from others is an attempt to protect yourself from vulnerability, yet it leaves you suffering in isolation like the child who grows up without a *good enough parent*. As a child, Justin learned how to maintain distance from others to avoid any risk of hurt, rejection, or shame. He also learned how to be self-sufficient to the point where it was excruciating for him to ask for help. His life-changing decision to start therapy and attend a twelve-step program is a meaningful path toward exploring emotionally reliable, deeply connected relationships.

Face it. We all long for love yet push it away at times. This is the human condition. So how can you learn about this part of you? Be curious. Don't judge yourself. Instead, notice when you create distance from others. By observing yourself nonjudgmentally, you give yourself the room to be fully you. Ask yourself what purpose distancing serves and the reason for it.

**Action Step**: Take a look at your intimacy patterns and identify times when you avoid getting closer to the other person. This may require the help of a therapist as you track relationships or experiences when you avoid intimacy consciously or unconsciously. Hint: Begin with your family of origin as a clue to where these patterns developed.

**Action Step**: Get to know your intimacy template. How was love and intimacy expressed among family members? For instance, I can't remember the "L-word" ever being spoken in my childhood home. My family norm was withholding and avoidant. How was love and intimacy expressed between your parents (if they were together when you were a child)? Because I have very little recollection of my parents showing love to one another, I had little or no role modeling of intimacy and affection.

_____

_____

_____

**Action Step**: Identify any extended family, friends, teachers, or pets who were sources of love. If love wasn't readily expressed or available in your childhood, where were your sources or role models for intimacy? For instance, I am forever grateful for my grandmother and my Siberian husky, Nikki, who were effusive with love that provided me with a deep experience of intimacy.

_____

_____

_____

**Action Step:** List any boundary crossings or intrusions. Boundaries are a vital component of love based in mutual trust and mutual respect. How were boundaries respected or not in your family? Did a parent use you as a confidant because they were unhappy in their marriage?

_____

_____

_____

**Awareness Step:** Listen to your nervous system. Feeling over-activated by too much closeness indicates *intimacy overload* and can be alleviated by regulating the emotional distance. Because my mom's needs felt overpowering to me as a young child, I felt smothered and disconnected from its true impact. Today I know that I have the choice to say "yes, no, or maybe" to avoid intrusive relationships. Now I only experience echoes of helplessness and feel more regulated to choose what feels right to me. Notice if you tend to shut down, disconnect, or possibly get highly anxious or even rageful.

If you have love-avoidant tendencies, and most of us do, there is nothing wrong with you. Remember that it's not a disease, and it's not pathological. You are not broken, but you may have some leftover brokenheartedness from childhood. Stay curious about it and ask for help from a professional or a trusted confidant. It takes courage and vulnerability to take the risk to be fully yourself—love-avoidance and all.

## Relying on the Reliable

Early attachment patterns begin with the baby longing for the gleam in the eye from the parent or caregiver. The gleam lets the child know they are a precious, valuable human being. We all have a deep wish to be loved and valued from the time we're born, and being seen as a lovable, desirable person sets the stage for the possibility of trust, respect, and intimacy along the lifespan. If all these necessary ingredients are present, you're on your way to emotionally nourishing connections.

**Action Step:** Who provided the gleam in the eye for you when you were a child? If you can't identify anyone, who provides the gleam today? And who would you like to express the gleam in their eye to you?

_____

_____

_____

In his book, *Addiction as an Attachment Disorder*, Dr. Philip Flores explores the fundamental role of attachment as applied to substance abuse, and his theories can also be applied to sexual compulsivity. He describes addiction as "a condition of isolation which often originates with insecure attachments. Not everyone with inadequate attachment experiences will become addicted, but everyone with an addiction suffers with attachment difficulties. Addiction occurs when the attachment to a behavior or a substance becomes stronger than the attachment to people and caring, loving, nurturing relationships." With out-of-control sexual behavior, compulsive urges increase when the attachment to self-destructive behaviors remains stronger than the attachment to real relationships in your life. Therefore, true healing takes place when the attachment to intimate relationships overpowers the attachment to compulsive sex.

**Action Step:** Is your attachment to loving relationships greater than your attachment to compulsive sexual behavior? If so, elaborate. If not, say more about this.

_____

_____

_____

Accepting and exploring your desire for deeper connection with others is a foundation for emotional resilience and attachment repair. In American culture, which highly values autonomy, accepting the fact that you need others to survive is often overlooked. As a result, self-sufficiency is highly endorsed, and asking for help is often discouraged. When you learn to lean on dependable people, slowly but surely, the early attachment gaps fade, and emotional repair begins. Because you're biologically wired for connection, your brain will respond to the newly forming intimate pathways as a welcome change rather than a scary one. How do you do this? Through twelve-step involvement, psychotherapy, coaching, and volunteering, you'll have the opportunity to move toward community and belonging rather than perpetuating isolation and disconnection.

**Action Step**: Describe the ways you feel connected to others in your life. If you feel disconnected, describe this as well.

_____

_____

_____

Gradually, you'll learn to trust and internalize your recovery team—those you have chosen to invite into this chapter of your life. Remember that it's not about quantity but instead about quality. You get to pick your team, so choose wisely. By cultivating safe-enough, nurturing relationships, you'll be well on your way to living your life with contentment and love. Sprinkle in some meditation, exercise, and overall self-care and you'll fill your heart.

**Action Step:** Who is on your recovery team?

_____

_____

_____

**Action Step:** What role would you like them to play on your team?

_____

_____

_____

In summary, your long-term prognosis for sustainable recovery is dependent upon your capacity for more satisfying, nourishing relationships. Avoidant-attachment patterns are self-protective and purposeful, yet they are not set in stone. They are only reminders of what feels safer to you and what gets in the way of what you really want—unconditional love and belonging.

**Action Step:** Lean into safe, loving relationships gradually rather than avoiding them. Become the pursuer rather than the distancer. Who would you like to pursue as a friend or confidant? Consider your options and choose one relationship to pursue.

_____

_____

_____

**Action Step:** Be a giver of love even if it's scary, uncharted territory. Notice when love shows up in front of you and take note of how it feels on the inside. Track loving moments—both giving love to others and receiving love from others.

_____

_____

_____

**Awareness Step:** Learn from your pets. They are instinctive teachers of unconditional love, acceptance, and play. If you have a pet, pay attention to their unconditional love and acceptance. Savor it. If you don't have a pet, consider fostering one or volunteering at your local shelter.

**Action Step:** Take inventory of the most intimate friendships in your life. Write a list of your past relationships that have been most meaningful. Identify their commonalities.

_____

_____

_____

**Awareness Step:** Notice when you feel more trust and relaxation in relationships. Without these qualities present, intimacy doesn't exist. Be mindful when you're feeling more relaxed with others. Take note of what happens inside of you and how this indicates deepening trust.

**Action Step:** Identify *your people* and cultivate these nourishing relationships.

_____

_____

_____

## Lori's Story: Identifying Love Addiction

*Lori arrived for therapy with tears in her eyes. "I did it again. I fell for another guy who was totally unavailable and once again convinced myself that he was the one. I don't know if I can go through this again. I am so humiliated." I had been treating Lori for the past year, and we've been tracking her tendency to merge with guys she didn't know very well and proceed to build elaborate fantasies about them. Although she was well aware of this painful pattern, Lori kept falling into this emotional quicksand.*

*"My parents split up when I was eight, and my dad quickly started a new family. Ever since my parents divorced, I felt like I was the stepchild as he paid way more*

*attention to my stepmother and her kids. Don't get me wrong. I was glad the fighting between my parents finally came to an end, but I was also extremely jealous of my stepsiblings. They got way more of my father than I ever did. Nowadays when I get involved with a boyfriend, I tend to take him hostage and secretly hope that he will be my knight in shining armor who has arrived to rescue me.*

The term "love addiction" is deceiving. It's not about love—it's about the fantasy of love which often snowballs into obsession. Here are some of its primary characteristics:

- Fear of abandonment.
- Fear of intimacy.
- Emotionally unreliable parent(s).
- Desire to be rescued.
- Attracted to love avoidants.
- Elaborate romantic fantasy.
- After fantasy lifts, a period of withdrawal.

Love addiction usually stems from anxious-ambivalent attachment patterns from childhood. When a parent is neglectful, children blame themselves and feel there is something inherently wrong with them. Typically, at least one parent is emotionally unreliable and abandoning, and in Lori's case she had a father who deserted her for his new wife and family. Lori's father hunger—her desire to be seen, heard, and understood by a man—was profound.

During a full-blown romantic fantasy, the brain gets hijacked as it latches on to the idea of being rescued. The brain gets stuck in an obsessive loop and cannot break free from it. Although Lori is a capable, competent woman in other areas of her life, in love relationships her unmet longings take over and she turns into a heat-seeking missile. In her most recent scenario, she finally broke out of the obsession when she learned that her supposedly monogamous boyfriend was sleeping with several other women throughout their six-month relationship. Her fantasy bubble burst.

*When Lori turned thirty, her desire for intimate relationships was growing and her brokenheartedness was palpable. Our therapeutic relationship became a touchstone for her, and she intentionally sought me out as a male therapist because of her abandonment feelings related to her father. Although Lori wanted to trust me, she often tested me to see if I would criticize or abandon her. I viewed these tests as necessary ways for Lori to experience a reparative attachment experience with a consistent, reliable man and to know that we could talk about all her feelings. We made a pact that if she felt disappointed or fearful in our relationship, she would let me know. It was vital for her to know that inevitably I would let her down one way or another, but most importantly, we could process her reactions and feelings together.*

Is love addiction real? Lori's story demonstrates both the suffering and healing associated with deep attachment ruptures that resulted in her version of love addiction or anxious attachment style.

Now that Lori is recognizing the themes and patterns of her deeper longings, what are the tools and strategies she might consider?

1. Consider the following supports: psychotherapist, coach, sponsor, Higher Power, and emotionally reliable friends.
2. If you're not able to trust your gut instincts, rely on a dependable confidant to help recognize your fantasy patterns more clearly and efficiently. Practice humility and ask your confidants for help when you need it.
3. Going through withdrawal is a real phenomenon which occurs after the intoxicating effects of the fantasy are behind you. Know that this is a necessary phase of healing. Be kind and patient with your adjustment from fantasy to reality.
4. Find a relational therapist who thoroughly understands the intricacies of these entrenched fantasy patterns. Ask friends for referrals or shop around to find the right fit for you.
5. Group therapy can be a tremendous resource. It's usually best to wait until you're out of crisis, but once you feel ready, a group experience can be a very rich way to learn more extensively about yourself as you help others learn about themselves.
6. Sex and Love Addicts Anonymous is a twelve-step fellowship focusing on the integration of sex and intimacy. By attending a meeting, you will already feel less alone in your pain. And if you hang around long enough, you can develop dependable relationships with those who have gone through similar suffering.
7. When you're in fantasy, you will often feel expansive but quite ungrounded. When you're feeling better, the most powerful state you can experience is both expansive and grounded. Build awareness to know when you are feeling regulated or dysregulated. Savor your calm, peaceful, and grounded internal state.
8. Learn how to date in a calm, soothing way. If dating feels turbulent, it's not the right time. If you're using dating apps, find an accountability person so you can check in regularly with the fantasies that inevitably show up.
9. Meditation is one of the best anti-anxiety strategies available. Begin by using a meditation or relaxation app or try some guided self-compassion meditations. This will help you build a tone setter for each day as you learn to listen to the rhythm within.

## Sophia's Story: Allowing Obsession to be a Teacher

*She woke up every morning thinking about Julia and went to bed each night fantasizing about her. As much as she wanted to focus on other things, Sophia's thoughts would return to Julia like a magnet. By the time Sophia found her way to my office, she looked depleted and felt like she was losing her mind.*

*I reassured her that she wasn't going crazy, but I told her that her brain had been hijacked by the obsession of Julia. Although this was going to be a gradual withdrawal, Sophia seemed to accept her anguish as a symptom of what can be described as love addiction or romantic idealization.*

Sophia was drowning in fantasy and projections. She was lost in a rescue fantasy because Julia was older and financially stable and seemed to symbolize someone who would take care of her and save her from what she described as her lonely, boring life—a common fantasy. Although the earlier moments of obsession were exciting and pleasurable at times, it had snowballed into agonizing ruminations.

Obsession is universal as we all get obsessed with someone at one time or another. It's a by-product of deeper longings being activated. Obsession serves a purpose as it gives you the hope that you will feel better by getting together with this person or by getting something from this person. Unfortunately, this is a myth. The mind falls hook, line, and sinker into this distortion, and the torment deepens.

So, what might be the purpose of obsession? It's an opportunity to learn about life, learn about your mind and learn about your identity. Obsession is extremely useful, and there's really nothing quite like it in life. Pain grabs your attention, and sometimes you'll even get *addicted to misery*. Not only does this happen with romantic relationships but also with friends, family, or colleagues.

How can you connect it to something productive and use it throughout your life, now and in the future? The romantically obsessed person desperately wants something from the idealized other. It's generally not a conscious experience, but instead, a deep hunger as primitive longings are awakened. When the idealized other is not readily available, this often leaves the obsessed person in acute anxiety and despair as the other person falls short and cannot fulfill the depth of these desires.

Then the obsessive person leans even further into the fantasy, loses their identity, and carries the belief that happiness and stability is solely based on what the idealized person does or does not do. As a result, it's ungrounding and dysregulating often resulting in symptoms such as insomnia, panic attacks, and even rage.

Obsession is based in shame or the experience of "not being enough." Waiting for just the right level of contact from the other person is an attempt to find soothing. This is also what a baby longs for from their primary caregiver—being attended to in just the right way, at just the right time, at just the right temperature. If the fantasy person (or parent) doesn't respond in these idealized ways, it often results in profound hurt, intolerable fear, and inconsolable grief.

Here are some possible ways to give the obsessive mind something productive to do:

**Action Step:** Because obsession is a growth opportunity unlike any other, be curious and open-hearted about what it's trying to tell you. Develop an inventory of past obsessive relationships dating back to childhood.

_____

_____

_____

**Action Step:** Practice Mindful Self-Compassion which will give you a space to observe the mind nonjudgmentally. Listen to self-compassion guided meditations daily.

**Action Step:** Ask for help from others. Who is emotionally reliable in your life? Double up on your contact with these people.

---

---

---

**Action Step:** Work with a psychotherapist who fully understands obsession, romantic idealization, and love addiction. Disentangle the obsessive patterns of the past and train your brain to recognize and savor love.

**Action Step:** Visit the Sex and Love Addicts Anonymous website at www.slaa fws.org. Go to a meeting and listen with an open heart.

**Key Action Step:** Ask yourself: What do I really want from the other person? Once you've identified what you want, consider ways to bestow that upon yourself. *Sense what's missing in you based on what you want from them.*

---

---

---

**Key Action Step:** How can I become more of a "giver" rather than a "taker"? Instead of getting stuck in the hunger of wanting, what do I have to give? The Prayer of Saint Francis describes this internal shift. Recite the prayer out loud daily and see how it resonates for you.

---

---

---

**The Prayer of Saint Francis**
*Lord,* make me an instrument of thy peace.
Where there is hatred, let me sow love;
Where there is injury, pardon;
Where there is doubt, faith;
Where there is despair, hope;
Where there is darkness, light;
Where there is sadness, joy.
*O divine Master,* grant that I may not so much seek
To be consoled as to console,
To be understood as to understand,

To be loved as to love;
For it is in giving that we receive;
It is in pardoning that we are pardoned;
It is in dying to self that we are born to eternal life.
   (Note: *Lord & Divine Master* can be replaced with *Universal Energy, Higher Power, Goddess*, or whatever language fits your belief system.)

**Key Action Step:** Practice this five-step awareness process described below. Build it into a daily ritual possibly as a morning tone setter:

1. Visualize the other person as happy.
2. Identify your expectations for this person.
3. Locate the longing or desire in yourself that sets up this expectation.
4. Ask for the willingness to do whatever is necessary to bring about change in your attitude or attitudes?
5. Repeat over and over to yourself:
   - *I accept the other person exactly the way they are at any given moment.*
   - *I accept myself fully for exactly who I am at any given moment.*

Obsession is not a life sentence. If you're willing to illuminate the blind spots of the past, it will get easier. It may take some time to feel more like yourself again but be patient. It will get better if you gently unlock the mind and open the aperture to a larger, healing perspective over the course of time.

## Moving from Isolation to Intimacy

As we wind down this chapter, let's be clear about the purpose of avoidance. There is nothing inherently wrong with it. Sometimes it's a survival strategy and sometimes it's a way of pacing oneself. Do your best not to shame yourself for this attachment pattern.

**Action Step:** Describe how avoidance has served a purpose in your life.

_____

_____

_____

It's impossible to move quickly and easily from an avoidant attachment style into intimate relationships. Yet, it challenges you to lean into safe enough relationships when you feel relaxed and trusting enough of the other person. It's always a risk, but it's also the only way to find out if true intimacy is available.

Now that you have been getting to know your avoidant tendencies, it's time to have the agency to decide when, with whom and how close you choose to get to others. Coming from where you've been, it's vital to take all the time you need to enter the world of intimacy.

**Action Step:** Identify a relationship that you would like to gently pursue (romantic, friendship, family).

_____

_____

_____

After you take responsibility for your avoidant tendencies, you get to choose how close or how far you want to be from others. It's an opportunity to clarify boundaries—knowing where you end, and the other person begins. Ask yourself how involved you want to be in each relationship. Boundaries are respectful ways to determine how close you want to be with others and how much you choose to share about yourself. They also help you decide how close you allow others to be to you.

Deeper connection takes place when you take emotional risks and become vulnerable with others—the birthplace of intimacy. But only a select few people will have the honor of getting to know you in this authentic way. When you were compulsive, boundaries were either messy or sometimes non-existent. Chances are you never thought about boundaries or regulating the emotional distance when you were at the peak of your compulsivity. Boundaries are mutually respectful and help both parties have full choice on regulating the emotional distance. Receiving love requires a clear channel of respect, trust, and patience.

## Your Practice

1. Attachment styles develop early on with our original caregivers, so they were established from the beginning. Know that they can be understood and recalibrated through your loving relationships today.
2. Intimacy avoidance or avoidant attachment styles are self-protective and create a way to regulate the emotional distance from others. Consider the possibility of more intimacy in your life to create new neural pathways.
3. Cultivate the emotionally dependable relationships in your life. You can begin with a therapist or a coach to learn what it feels like to be unconditionally understood.
4. Breaking through the barriers that get in the way of secure attachment takes shape when you become more interested in emotionally honest relationships than your compulsive sexual behavior. Find the reliable-enough people in your life to help you repair the ruptures of your past.
5. Obsession may seem like a problem on the surface but can also be a valuable way to get to know deeper parts of yourself. Stay curious and nonjudgmental rather than self-attacking or shaming.

## References

Bauer, Jan. 2013. *Impossible Love: Or Why the Heart Must Go Wrong*. Brattleboro, VT: Echo Point Books.

Flores, Philip J. 2011. *Addiction as an Attachment Disorder*. Lanham, MD: Jason Aronson.

Winnicott, D.W. 1993. *The Child, the Family and the Outside World*. New York: Penguin.

# 10 Revitalizing Sexual Health

As someone who identifies both as a recovering sexual compulsive as well as a therapist, I've witnessed a lot of suffering as well as courageous healing. Yet, the phrase *sexual health* is rarely spoken. Why is this the case? It seems that there tends to be much more focus on overcoming problematic sexual behaviors rather than developing a fun, pleasurable, deeply connected sex life. As a result, the sustainability of long-term sexual recovery is not always addressed through the lens of sexual health, and it becomes an afterthought rather than a focal point.

**Action Step:** Sexual expression is a key to life fulfillment. Based on your personal relationship with sex, define sexual health.

_____

_____

_____

Although I've been familiar with the WHO definition for many years, its significance only came to my attention recently as part of a workshop I attended that was given by my talented colleagues, Douglas Braun-Harvey and Michael Vigorito. They have developed a non-pathologizing, affirming and forward-thinking sexual health model that destigmatizes compulsive sexual behavior and celebrates movement toward greater sexual expression. I believe this approach is a missing link toward creating more liberating, conscious sexual health as part of long-term recovery.

In their book, *Treating Out-of-Control Sexual Behaviors: Rethinking Sex Addiction*, Braun-Harvey and Vigorito define OCSB as a "sexual problem of consensual urges, thoughts, or behaviors that feel out of control for the individual." They go on to say that "sexual health conversations matter." Their open-hearted approach was developed after many years of working with their clients who buried their sexual stories rather than through open and inquisitive exploration.

They have developed a clinically sound treatment approach allowing individuals to determine if they have a problem and to determine the client's level of motivation to work on their behavior. Rather than labeling it or using typical "disease model" language with their clients, they look for ways to bring out the integrity of the individual while promoting a shift from secretive behaviors to

DOI: 10.4324/9781032650487-11

transparency. This usually takes place within the context of individual sessions as well as a weekly sexual health men's group.

Braun-Harvey and Vigorito believe that ending your existing relationship with out-of-control sexual behaviors is not supposed to be about deprivation; instead, it's about reclaiming one's birthright as a sexual being. They also believe that the challenges individuals face with OCSB has to do with 1. Attachment ruptures 2. Nervous system dysregulation and 3. Erotic conflicts. Let's explore these three elements:

*Attachment rupture:* severe gaps in attachment bonds, typically in early childhood.

Because my mother had difficulty attuning to me, there was a large gap between what I needed and what I received.

**Action Step:** Do you identify with an attachment gap? If so, how?

_____

_____

_____

*Nervous system regulation:* over-reacting or under-reacting to experiences or situations usually caused by unresolved stress or trauma from the past.

Fluctuating from regulation to dysregulation is part of being human, but if you are dysregulated much of the time, you will be much more vulnerable to compulsive sexual behavior. Because I fluctuated from anxious to depressed (i.e., up regulated to down regulated), my nervous system was not accustomed to being in a regulated state or in a calmer, more peaceful state. Eventually this led to my problematic sexual behavior which was actually an attempt to regulate my system.

**Action Step:** How do you see your nervous system as either regulated or dysregulated historically? Describe your experience of being more regulated or more dysregulated through the years?

_____

_____

_____

*Erotic conflict:* a person engages in sexual activity which conflicts with their values, whether they be moral, spiritual, or religious. In the past I tried to conform to heterosexual norms such as marriage and monogamy, and as a result I don't know if I ever gave myself the freedom to consider other possibilities. For example, I consistently have honest conversations with clients about monogamy and other sexual desires. The aperture has opened for these discussions, yet it also creates erotic conflicts for some clients.

**Action Step:** Do you identify any lingering erotic conflicts? If so, elaborate.

_____

_____

_____

### Defying Shame-Based Sexuality

Shame-based sexuality usually begins in childhood in our families, schools, religious institutions, and neighborhoods.

**Action Step:** What associations to shame-based sexuality do you experience?

_____

_____

_____

**Action Step:** What messages about sexuality did you receive from your family?

_____

_____

_____

**Action Step:** What messages about sexuality did you receive in your school or neighborhood from teachers or peers?

_____

_____

_____

**Action Step:** If your family was affiliated with a religious or spiritual institution, what messages about sexuality did you receive from these places of worship or how did your family interpret them?

_____

_____

_____

Where did you get your sex education? In the pre-HIV world of the 1970s, my public school "health teacher" arrived in my sixth-grade class and showed us colorful slides of body parts that were anatomically correct but rather one-dimensional and confusing. There was little or no discussion about intercourse, contraception, or masturbation—and of course nothing related to same-gender sex. As I understand it, things really haven't changed much in the past forty-five years, and the idea of sexual pleasure is not commonly discussed.

## Otis's Story: Learning Sex Education

*In the Netflix series* Sex Education, *the protagonist, Otis, is a curious teenager whose mother is a sex therapist with a home office where she offers seminars focusing on the wonders of the vulva. Vicariously, Otis picks up on some of her sexual wisdom and expertise, and he is dubbed the "sex kid" at school. He opens an underground business to dispense advice to his naive but sexually active cohorts. Although Otis is initially a virgin himself, he tries to reassure others in the school and does so with moderate success.*

The lack of sex education from families and schools often leaves kids with misconceptions and profound isolation. How might this be different?

Here we will look at some strategies that most of us were not given as teenagers. As mentioned earlier, sexual health is one missing link of sexual recovery, and it's never too late to invest in your sex education.

In my early experience and exposure to sexuality, it wasn't something that was talked about. Sex education was limited to learning parts of the anatomy, but actual sex and sexuality seemed like a taboo subject to discuss. Therefore, sex and secrecy became over coupled for me.

**Action Step**: What did you learn about sex and sexuality in your sex education class?

_____

_____

_____

**Action Step:** How did you learn about sex and sexuality?

_____

_____

_____

There is no cookie-cutter approach to healing from sexual compulsivity, but one thing I do know: There is still a lot of anguish, and sexual health conversations with qualified individuals offer a refreshing, nonjudgmental way to face these problematic behaviors with curiosity. Rather than a one-size-fits-all method, think about sexual health as an essential dimension of your well-being.

## Reviving Pleasure

"Pleasure" is a word that is often overlooked in the twelve-step rooms. Instead, there is a focus on what's wrong or what's missing. We're going to turn things around and look at what's right and what could be even better.

It's been a few hundred years since Puritanical beliefs thrived in early America when sex for pleasure was seen as morally wrong. Yet, religious dogma continues to exist in our society today, and some faith communities still contribute to confusion and shame based on rigid, outdated rules such as prohibition of same-sex practices as well as sex before marriage.

Fortunately, religious rigidity is not as pervasive today, but for many, our sexual attitudes and behaviors remain constricted.

With an emphasis on "positive and respectful" as well as "pleasurable and safe sexual experiences," the universally accepted definition of sexual health demonstrates how far we have come on an international level, but we still have a long way to go. Here is the story of Jack, which illustrates the common way teenagers often stumble into their sexual awakening:

## Jack's Story: Experiencing a Sexual Awakening

*By the time Jack arrived in my therapy office in his early twenties, he knew he craved real-life sex. He expressed his desire to date and explore with someone other than images on the screen. Jack's teenage porn use was a common story and often becomes an introduction to sex and sexual turn-ons.*

*Raised in a liberal Methodist home, Jack was twelve years old when he stumbled upon his father's porn stash. Immediately, Jack was hooked, and his young brain started to crave more elaborate forms of porn which interfered with his interest in dating. "Internet porn seemed so much easier than meeting a girl," he confided early in his therapy. In addition to porn, he used edibles to enhance his sexual experiences and this "pot and porn" ritual became a daily habit. Although sexual pleasure was gratifying at times, he felt increasingly lonely and empty.*

In the early twentieth century Carl Jung described the necessity to embrace the shadow within us in order to fully experience our lighter parts. Regarding sex, shame, or censorship of one's sexual self creates a barrier to pleasure, and there is already more than enough sexual shame in most of us. Instead, how can Jack learn about his sexual identity and choices based on pleasurable, respectful, and safe sexual experiences? Although compulsive porn use was not a sustainable activity for him, it was the catalyst for Jack to learn about his body and his sexual turn-ons, as well as his sense of pleasure.

Jung might describe Jack's behavior part of his shadow self because it's secretive, but it also opens the door to lighter aspects of sex—fun, play and freedom. The *Merriam-Webster Dictionary* defines pleasure as "a state of gratification; a source of delight or joy." As a sexual being, pleasurable sex is your birthright, yet *self-pleasure* is rarely discussed. Once again, the echoes of the Puritans may get in the way of this human desire which may be defined as follows: *any experience that brings you closer to contentment, relaxation, or serenity.* Examples of self-pleasure—sexual or sensual—include masturbation, a hot bath, massage, facial, or giving yourself a hug or sensual touch.

Pleasure is not only a concept—it's an action. Here we will look at specific ways to safely explore pleasure as a strategy for long-term freedom and sexual satisfaction.

**Action Step**: When you think about the word "pleasure," what are your immediate associations that go along with it? Write down all thoughts, feelings, images, and memories, and be sure to remain curious and nonjudgmental.

_____

_____

_____

**Action Step:** Define the word "pleasure" for yourself. Your private ideas and beliefs about pleasure will help you develop a sexual vision.

_____

_____

_____

**Action Step:** What are the messages from childhood that get in the way of your freedom and enjoyment of pleasure? These messages may come from family, friends, school, community, and religious organizations. List as many of these messages that may have become stubborn barriers to pleasure.

_____

_____

_____

**Action Step:** What are the messages from childhood that encouraged pleasure? List as many of these messages that were "pleasure positive."

_____

_____

_____

**Action Step:** What gives you pleasure? Without overthinking it, brainstorm and make a list of pleasurable experiences you already enjoy—both sexual and non-sexual.

_____

_____

_____

**Action Step**: In our society, self-pleasure is often a taboo subject. As discussed in part one of this section, you can expand self-pleasure to mean anything that brings you contentment, relaxation, or serenity. What are the ways that you self-soothe? Do you enjoy a hot bath? Do you have a favorite type of music you listen to? Take your time to list those items that you already do and the items you would like to add to your toolbox of self-pleasure activities.

_____

_____

_____

**Action Step:** Sexual health includes safe, positive, respectful, and pleasurable experiences. What sexual experiences are safe, respectful, and pleasurable whether it be with another person or by yourself? Once you consider sexual activities that are fun, playful, and liberating, share this list with a confidant or trusted professional.

_____

_____

_____

**Action Step:** Is there residual shame connected to your sexual expression? Sexual shame gets in the way of being in the moment and feeling sexual freedom. Consider individual, group therapy, or twelve-step meetings to build shame resiliency. Find a confidant or a group to share these parts of you that create this unnecessary burden. Find the courage to break out of the secrecy and expand your sexual voice.

_____

_____

_____

Because sexual hang-ups and barriers are so prevalent, it takes courage to investigate your sexual health and freely explore what's pleasurable. Unlike the Puritans, sexual liberation is yours to discover. Take your time with these suggested action steps because it takes a while to un-do a lifetime of unhelpful messages and sexual barriers. It often takes a team of open-hearted, unconditional therapists, coaches, sponsors, and confidants to mend the brokenheartedness that goes along with sexual wounds, and it often requires the right healers to help you thrive as a sexual being. Remember, the more you explore the shadow, the more the light will shine brightly.

A few years ago, I attended a presentation given by a "pleasure researcher." I had never met anyone who wrote their dissertation about *pleasure,* and I found it rather refreshing and hopeful. It seems to me that pleasure is generally not something that gets a lot of airtime. Instead, pain and trauma dominate the halls of research. I believe we still live in a culture here in America that suffers from the echoes of Puritanical beliefs or rigid morality.

**Action Step:** What has given you pleasure in the past?

_____

_____

_____

**Action Step:** What has given you sexual pleasure in the past?

_____

_____

_____

**Action Step:** What gives you pleasure in your life today?

_____

_____

_____

## Playing with Healthier Fantasy

Fantasy gets a bad rap in the twelve-step rooms because there is a primary emphasis on *living life on life's terms* and staying firmly in reality. But what's wrong with letting your imagination run wild and playing in your rolodex of fantasies? If fantasy is safe enough, it's worth considering. If fantasy has been problematic or leaves you in some kind of conflict, it's probably not so productive for your recovery. Consulting with a sponsor or a therapist may give you more agency over your fantasy world.

## Considering Fantasy as a Survival Strategy

Fantasy is defined as "imagination, especially when extravagant and unrestrained" (www.dictionary.com), and it can also be a liberating exploration of your wants and desires, both sexual and romantic. Is it possible that fantasy can be safe and productive? Can your imagination, even if *extravagant or unrestrained*, be integrated into your revised sexual health plan?

The answer is yes, and no. Fantasy can simply be a safe voyage into your wildest dreams, or it can be a survival strategy to transcend painful and overwhelming circumstances. For example, you know by now that I grew up in an emotionally unstable and sometimes turbulent home. As a kid, I was a TV-holic and many of my favorite shows such as *The Wonderful World of Disney*, *Happy Days* and *The Love Boat* served as mini-vacations from the reality of my family. I eagerly looked forward to Saturday night at nine to discover the guest celebrities on *The Love Boat* and *Fantasy Island* as they travelled to exotic destinations. This weekly escape was the perfect remedy for a young child stuck in a family overflowing with misery.

*At first, fantasy served a purpose in my childhood, but as an adult it became out of control at times, leading to highly obsessive thoughts, compulsive behaviors, and negative consequences. In my case, it started very innocently. My best friend became my first romantic interest at age five. At the time I had no understanding of the depth of the fantasy, but he seemed to have a loving family who adopted me and became one of the many surrogate families in my childhood. As part of my survival, I always had a best friend who became the object of my affection, admiration, and fantasy at times.*

*When I reached puberty, sexual fantasy kicked into full gear and although innocent at first, it unraveled into more obsessive and compulsive behaviors into my young adult years. I didn't realize this at the time, but my young, impressionable brain was hyper focused on painful obsessive longings, both romantic and sexual. Fantasy had become agonizing.*

On the other hand, I feel fortunate that my coming-of-age years unfolded before the invention of the Internet because the epidemic of fantasy has exploded exponentially with the advent of internet porn and dating apps. We now know that incessant porn and app use leads to overdeveloped brain circuitry toward these behaviors. Neural pathways get habituated to the search for the perfect person or body part which may result in a distortion of reality as well as obsession. For some, unrestrained fantasy takes over and leads to unexpected consequences.

Recently, a young male client told me that he is only able to climax with porn images but not with actual sexual partners. He is interested in real-life sex but has been hooked on porn for the past ten years. We now call this *porn-induced erectile dysfunction*. The brain-body connection has acclimated to these images and doesn't recognize the body cues to get stimulated with a real person. Not only does this cause him shame and humiliation with his girlfriend, but he now realizes he is suffering both emotional and sexual intimacy consequences from his compulsive relationship to porn. The good news is that he is seeking help, acknowledging his problem, and realizing that porn has been his survival strategy from a family where he felt unseen and neglected by overburdened, distant parents. Fantasy always serves a purpose, but it can lead to unforeseen troubles if it overshadows reality.

The following action steps are separated into two distinct areas:

1. Fantasy as an ally.
2. Fantasy as an obsession.

## Fantasy as an Ally

**Awareness Step:** Don't pathologize fantasy. Be curious, nonjudgmental, and open-hearted. Allow fantasy to be a teacher and simply a part of who you are. Give yourself the opportunity to consider fantasy as an ally.

**Action Step:** List your romantic fantasies from as far back as you can remember. Are they pleasant? Unpleasant? Neutral? Notice what it feels like to take a closer look at your rolodex of fantasy memories. If you feel too activated or overwhelmed, take a break and discuss this exercise with a trusted confidant when you feel more regulated.

_____

_____

_____

**Action Step**: List your sexual fantasies from childhood to now.

_____

_____

_____

**Action Step:** How has fantasy served a purpose in your life? What have been the benefits of fantasy, both romantic and sexual? How have these fantasies been a useful part of your imagination? How have they been a survival strategy?

_____

_____

_____

**Action Step:** Sexual fantasy is part of your erotic template and part of your life energy. Celebrate your sexual self. List your fantasies here and share them with a therapist, sponsor, or sex coach. If you have a partner, share your fantasies with them. Liberate yourself from keeping that part of you under wraps. If you don't have a partner, take stock of your sexual fantasies, and know that they are part of a sexual playground to be explored.

**Action Step:** Express gratitude for your fantasies.

## Fantasy as Obsession

**Action Step:** Has romantic fantasy become obsessive for you resulting in negative consequences? If so, list the obsessive fantasies as well as the consequences associated with each fantasy.

_____

_____

_____

**Action Step:** Has sexual fantasy become obsessive and resulted in negative consequences? If so, list the sexual fantasies that have resulted in negative consequences.

_____

_____

_____

**Action Step:** What is your relationship to on-line porn and are you aware of any problems your porn use has caused? If so, explore how porn has been a barrier to intimacy as well as face to face relationships?

_____

_____

_____

**Action Step:** What is your relationship to dating apps? Do you find yourself getting lost in the world of apps and swiping for the perfect person or perfect body parts? Again, notice how these habits interfere with the integration of sex and intimacy in your life?

_____

_____

_____

**Awareness Step:** Fantasy can be a very self-centered activity where the brain gets hyper focused on immediate gratification. Consider other-centered activities.

Fantasy is a vital part of your life energy and your imagination. Don't hide from or eliminate safe, productive ways to fantasize and have fun. If it does feel out of control, seek professional help from a sexual health expert who understands the complicated underpinnings often rooted in relational trauma. Obsessive, compulsive fantasy is not a life sentence but requires attention to minimize future harm.

**Action Step:** Take an inventory of your go-to fantasies. Believe it or not, I had a poster of Farrah Fawcett in my bedroom which was a misguided example of my early sexual fantasy.

_____

_____

_____

**Action Step:** How would you describe your primary sexual fantasies? Try not to edit them but simply take a curious look at what they express to you.

_____

_____

_____

**Action Step:** How has fantasy been an ally for you? How has it given you pleasure?

_____

_____

_____

**Action Step:** How has fantasy been a problem for you? How has it caused difficulties?

_____

_____

_____

**Action Step:** What is your future vision of fun, liberating, sexual fantasy?

_____

_____

_____

**Action Step:** How would you like to explore your fantasies safely and productively?

_____

_____

_____

## Configuring Your Erotic Roadmap

Learning to identify when something results in inner conflict or inner peace will help you distinguish between items that belong in your erotic vision and those that do not. In addition to fantasy, your erotic roadmap may be a vulnerable part of your sexual self. As you answer these questions, find an unconditional person to walk beside you.

**Action Step:** Write an inventory of your most erotic memories, experiences, and desires from your past. Go into as much or as little detail as you want.

_____

_____

_____

**Action Step:** What are your current erotic desires? They may or may not align with the past. Hint: My current erotic desires are quite different from twenty to thirty years ago.

_____

_____

_____

**Action Step:** What do you consider to be your erotic fantasies and what do you consider to be your erotic realities?

_____

_____

_____

Action Step: How would you like to investigate and develop your future erotic roadmap?

_____

_____

_____

## Your Practice

1. Sexual health is a core aspect of your overall well-being. Prioritize it as a step toward more vitality and pleasure.
2. If you have been viewing porn images for many years, know that your brain and body need to recalibrate. It can take up to a year to physiologically shift from images on a screen to a real person in front of you. Exploring your sexual self is a brave new territory.
3. If you experience erectile problems without the use of porn, speak to a trusted physician or sexual health professional who can walk you through some steps to get to know your body again.

4. Sex therapists and sex coaches are trained to focus on sexual health issues. Sex addiction therapists are trained to focus on compulsive sexual behaviors. Ideally, find someone who is trained and certified in both areas. When sexual expression gets buried, it becomes more secretive and shameful resulting in unnecessary suffering.

5. Consider twelve-step support if you identify your issue as compulsive and persistent. You are biologically wired for connection, and twelve-step communities may provide a sense of belonging based on sharing a similar problem.

6. Once your sexual compulsivity has slowed down, ask your therapist to help you develop a Sexual Health Vision. Include pleasure, fantasy, and erotic desire as part of this honest conversation. You deserve a fun and liberating sex life.

7. Consider joining a therapy group with an emphasis on sexual health. Group therapy offers its members a powerful opportunity to build shame resiliency and camaraderie.

In conclusion, sexual health is often overlooked both in the twelve-step rooms, therapy offices and American culture in general, yet it's just as significant as mental health, emotional health, physical health, and spiritual health. Because puritanical ideas of sex are still pervasive in American culture, exploring your sexual health is a brave path of discovery as you find freedom beyond the compulsive sexual behavior of the past.

## References

Braun-Harvey, Douglas, and Michael Vigorito. 2015. *Treating Out-of-Control Sexual Behavior: Rethinking Sex Addiction*. New York: Springer.

Jung, C.J. 1966. *The Relations between the Ego and the Unconscious*. Oxfordshire: Routledge.

# Taking Your Practice on the Road

- Practice emotional resilience skills: relax, regulate, respond, relate.
- Accept grief as a teacher.
- Track moments of self-compassion and minimize self-attack.
- Embrace imperfection.
- Identify regulation vs. dysregulation.
- Breathe.
- Welcome solitude and stillness.
- Create contact with people and pets who regulate your nervous system.
- Discover what matters most to you.
- Investigate what gives your life meaning.
- Share gratitude.
- Contemplate forgiveness of self and others.
- Ask yourself what you really want and desire.
- Accept yourself for exactly who you are at any given moment.
- Practice other-centeredness and generosity of spirit.
- Cultivate pleasure and play.
- Consider fun, safe fantasy.
- Reduce sexual shame.
- Craft your sexual recovery vision.
- Discover intimacy with emotionally reliable people.
- Recognize all feelings as relevant but temporary.
- Build effective boundaries.
- Stay curious and non-judgmental.
- Ask for help.
- Receive love.

*Reminder: If you're driving across the country from New York to Los Angeles and you get a flat tire in Des Moines, it doesn't mean you have to go back to New York. Fix the tire and keep going, no matter how many repairs you need to make along the way.*

## Community Resources

*Twelve-Step Programs for Sexual Compulsivity*

Sex Addicts Anonymous (SAA) www.saa-recovery.org
Sex and Love Addicts Anonymous (SLAA) www.slaafws.org

Sexaholics Anonymous (SA) www.sa.org
Sexual Compulsives Anonymous (SCA) www.sca-recovery.org

*Twelve-Step Programs for Significant Others, Loved Ones, & Couples*

COSA www.cosa-recovery.org
S-Anon www.sanon.org
Recovering Couples Anonymous (RCA) www.recovering-couples.org

## Trauma Healing Resources

Brainspotting www.brainspotting.com
Sensorimotor Psychotherapy www.sensorimotorpsychotherapy.org
Eye Movement Desensitization and Reprocessing (EMDR) www.emdr.com
Somatic Experiencing Trauma Institute (SE) www.traumahealing.org
NeuroAffective Relational Model (NARM) www.narmtraining.com
Trauma Resource Institute (TRM) www.traumaresourceinstitute.com

## Additional Resources

American Association of Sexuality Educators, Counselors and Therapists
  (AASECT)
www.aasect.org
American Group Psychotherapy Association (AGPA)
www.agpa.org
International Coach Federation (ICF)
www.coachfederation.org
Society for the Advancement of Sexual Health (SASH)
www.sash.net

# Index

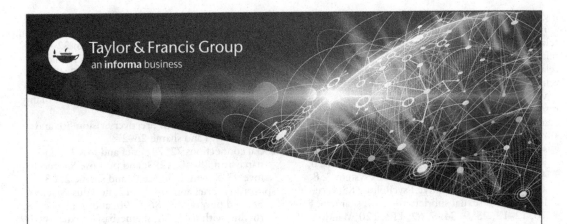

Printed in the United States
by Baker & Taylor Publisher Services